GOBLIN MARKET

GOBLIN MARKET

THE PRINCE'S PROGRESS AND OTHER POEMS

BY

CHRISTINA ROSSETTI

GYAN

Published by

Gyan Publishing House
5, Ansari Road
Daryaganj, New Delhi-110002
Phone: 011-47034999, 9811692060
E-mail: books@gyanbooks.com

Distribution Network
gyanbooks.com
India, USA, Canada, UK, Australia

ISBN: 978-81-212-5681-0 (PB)
First Published, 1879

2nd Impression 2024

Printed at: Gyan Press, Delhi.

GOBLIN MARKET
Author: CHRISTINA ROSSETTI

184

GOBLIN MARKET

THE PRINCE'S PROGRESS

AND OTHER POEMS

GOBLIN MARKET
THE PRINCE'S PROGRESS
AND OTHER POEMS

BY

CHRISTINA ROSSETTI

Geoffrey Cumberlege
OXFORD UNIVERSITY PRESS
London New York Toronto

TO

MY MOTHER

IN ALL REVERENCE AND LOVE

I INSCRIBE THIS BOOK

CONTENTS

Devotional Pieces

GOBLIN MARKET, AND OTHER POEMS, 1862

GOBLIN MARKET

MORNING and evening
Maids heard the goblins cry:
'Come buy our orchard fruits,
Come buy, come buy:
Apples and quinces,
Lemons and oranges,
Plump unpecked cherries,
Melons and raspberries,
Bloom-down-cheeked peaches,
Swart-headed mulberries,
Wild free-born cranberries,
Crab-apples, dewberries,
Pine-apples, blackberries,
Apricots, strawberries;—
All ripe together
In summer weather,—
Morns that pass by,
Fair eves that fly;
Come buy, come buy:
Our grapes fresh from the vine,
Pomegranates full and fine,

Dates and sharp bullaces,
Rare pears and greengages,
Damsons and bilberries,
Taste them and try:
Currants and gooseberries,
Bright-fire-like barberries,
Figs to fill your mouth,
Citrons from the South,
Sweet to tongue and sound to eye;
Come buy, come buy.'

Evening by evening
Among the brookside rushes,
Laura bowed her head to hear,
Lizzie veiled her blushes:
Crouching close together
In the cooling weather,
With clasping arms and cautioning lips,
With tingling cheeks and finger tips.
'Lie close,' Laura said,
Pricking up her golden head:
'We must not look at goblin men,
We must not buy their fruits:
Who knows upon what soil they fed
Their hungry thirsty roots?'
'Come buy,' call the goblins
Hobbling down the glen.
'Oh,' cried Lizzie, 'Laura, Laura,
You should not peep at goblin men.'
Lizzie covered up her eyes,

Covered close lest they should look ;
Laura reared her glossy head,
And whispered like the restless brook :
' Look, Lizzie, look, Lizzie,
Down the glen tramp little men.
One hauls a basket,
One bears a plate,
One lugs a golden dish
Of many pounds weight.
How fair the vine must grow
Whose grapes are so luscious ;
How warm the wind must blow
Through those fruit bushes.'
' No,' said Lizzie : ' No, no, no ;
Their offers should not charm us,
Their evil gifts would harm us.'
She thrust a dimpled finger
In each ear, shut eyes and ran :
Curious Laura chose to linger
Wondering at each merchant man.
One had a cat's face,
One whisked a tail,
One tramped at a rat's pace,
One crawled like a snail,
One like a wombat prowled obtuse and furry,
One like a ratel tumbled hurry skurry.
She heard a voice like voice of doves
Cooing all together :
They sounded kind and full of loves
In the pleasant weather.

Laura stretched her gleaming neck
Like a rush-imbedded swan,
Like a lily from the beck,
Like a moonlit poplar branch,
Like a vessel at the launch
When its last restraint is gone.

Backwards up the mossy glen
Turned and trooped the goblin men,
With their shrill repeated cry,
'Come buy, come buy.'
When they reached where Laura was
They stood stock still upon the moss,
Leering at each other,
Brother with queer brother;
Signalling each other,
Brother with sly brother.
One set his basket down,
One reared his plate;
One began to weave a crown
Of tendrils, leaves, and rough nuts brown
(Men sell not such in any town);
One heaved the golden weight
Of dish and fruit to offer her:
'Come buy, come buy,' was still their cry.
Laura stared but did not stir,
Longed but had no money:
The whisk-tailed merchant bade her taste
In tones as smooth as honey,
The cat-faced purr'd,

The rat-paced spoke a word
Of welcome, and the snail-paced even was heard ;
One parrot-voiced and jolly
Cried ' Pretty Goblin ' still for ' Pretty Polly ; '—
One whistled like a bird.

But sweet-tooth Laura spoke in haste :
' Good folk, I have no coin ;
To take were to purloin :
I have no copper in my purse,
I have no silver either,
And all my gold is on the furze
That shakes in windy weather
Above the rusty heather.'
' You have much gold upon your head,'
They answered all together :
' Buy from us with a golden curl.'
She clipped a precious golden lock,
She dropped a tear more rare than pearl,
Then sucked their fruit globes fair or red :
Sweeter than honey from the rock,
Stronger than man-rejoicing wine,
Clearer than water flowed that juice ;
She never tasted such before,
How should it cloy with length of use ?
She sucked and sucked and sucked the more
Fruits which that unknown orchard bore ;
She sucked until her lips were sore ;
Then flung the emptied rinds away
But gathered up one kernel stone,

And knew not was it night or day
As she turned home alone.

Lizzie met her at the gate
Full of wise upbraidings:
'Dear, you should not stay so late,
Twilight is not good for maidens;
Should not loiter in the glen
In the haunts of goblin men.
Do you not remember Jeanie,
How she met them in the moonlight,
Took their gifts both choice and many,
Ate their fruits and wore their flowers
Plucked from bowers
Where summer ripens at all hours?
But ever in the noonlight
She pined and pined away;
Sought them by night and day,
Found them no more but dwindled and grew grey;
Then fell with the first snow,
While to this day no grass will grow
Where she lies low:
I planted daisies there a year ago
That never blow.
You should not loiter so.'
'Nay, hush,' said Laura:
'Nay, hush, my sister:
I ate and ate my fill,
Yet my mouth waters still;
To-morrow night I will

Buy more:' and kissed her:
'Have done with sorrow;
I'll bring you plums to-morrow
Fresh on their mother twigs,
Cherries worth getting;
You cannot think what figs
My teeth have met in,
What melons icy-cold
Piled on a dish of gold
Too huge for me to hold,
What peaches with a velvet nap,
Pellucid grapes without one seed:
Odorous indeed must be the mead
Whereon they grow, and pure the wave they drink
With lilies at the brink,
And sugar-sweet their sap.'

Golden head by golden head,
Like two pigeons in one nest
Folded in each other's wings,
They lay down in their curtained bed:
Like two blossoms on one stem,
Like two flakes of new-fall'n snow,
Like two wands of ivory
Tipped with gold for awful kings.
Moon and stars gazed in at them,
Wind sang to them lullaby,
Lumbering owls forbore to fly,
Not a bat flapped to and fro
Round their nest:

Cheek to cheek and breast to breast
Locked together in one nest.

Early in the morning
When the first cock crowed his warning,
Neat like bees, as sweet and busy,
Laura rose with Lizzie :
Fetched in honey, milked the cows,
Aired and set to rights the house,
Kneaded cakes of whitest wheat,
Cakes for dainty mouths to eat,
Next churned butter, whipped up cream,
Fed their poultry, sat and sewed ;
Talked as modest maidens should :
Lizzie with an open heart,
Laura in an absent dream,
One content, one sick in part ;
One warbling for the mere bright day's delight,
One longing for the night.

At length slow evening came :
They went with pitchers to the reedy brook ;
Lizzie most placid in her look,
Laura most like a leaping flame.
They drew the gurgling water from its deep ;
Lizzie plucked purple and rich golden flags,
Then turning homewards said : 'The sunset flushes
Those furthest loftiest crags ;
Come, Laura, not another maiden lags,
No wilful squirrel wags,

The beasts and birds are fast asleep.'
But Laura loitered still among the rushes
And said the bank was steep.

And said the hour was early still,
The dew not fall'n, the wind not chill:
Listening ever, but not catching
The customary cry,
'Come buy, come buy,'
With its iterated jingle
Of sugar-baited words:
Not for all her watching
Once discerning even one goblin
Racing, whisking, tumbling, hobbling;
Let alone the herds
That used to tramp along the glen,
In groups or single,
Of brisk fruit-merchant men.

Till Lizzie urged, 'O Laura, come;
I hear the fruit-call but I dare not look:
You should not loiter longer at this brook:
Come with me home.
The stars rise, the moon bends her arc,
Each glowworm winks her spark,
Let us get home before the night grows dark:
For clouds may gather
Though this is summer weather,
Put out the lights and drench us through;
Then if we lost our way what should we do?'

Laura turned cold as stone
To find her sister heard that cry alone,
That goblin cry,
'Come buy our fruits, come buy.'
Must she then buy no more such dainty fruit?
Must she no more such succous pasture find,
Gone deaf and blind?
Her tree of life drooped from the root:
She said not one word in her heart's sore ache;
But peering thro' the dimness, nought discerning,
Trudged home, her pitcher dripping all the way;
So crept to bed, and lay
Silent till Lizzie slept;
Then sat up in a passionate yearning,
And gnashed her teeth for baulked desire, and wept
As if her heart would break.

Day after day, night after night,
Laura kept watch in vain
In sullen silence of exceeding pain.
She never caught again the goblin cry:
'Come buy, come buy;'—
She never spied the goblin men
Hawking their fruits along the glen:
But when the noon waxed bright
Her hair grew thin and grey;
She dwindled, as the fair full moon doth turn
To swift decay and burn
Her fire away.

One day remembering her kernel-stone
She set it by a wall that faced the south ;
Dewed it with tears, hoped for a root,
Watched for a waxing shoot,
But there came none ;
It never saw the sun,
It never felt the trickling moisture run :
While with sunk eyes and faded mouth
She dreamed of melons, as a traveller sees
False waves in desert drouth
With shade of leaf-crowned trees,
And burns the thirstier in the sandful breeze.

She no more swept the house,
Tended the fowls or cows,
Fetched honey, kneaded cakes of wheat,
Brought water from the brook :
But sat down listless in the chimney-nook
And would not eat.

Tender Lizzie could not bear
To watch her sister's cankerous care
Yet not to share.
She night and morning
Caught the goblins' cry :
'Come buy our orchard fruits,
Come buy, come buy : '—
Beside the brook, along the glen,
She heard the tramp of goblin men,
The voice and stir

Poor Laura could not hear ;
Longed to buy fruit to comfort her,
But feared to pay too dear.
She thought of Jeanie in her grave,
Who should have been a bride ;
But who for joys brides hope to have
Fell sick and died
In her gay prime,
In earliest Winter time,
With the first glazing rime,
With the first snow-fall of crisp Winter time.

Till Laura dwindling
Seemed knocking at Death's door :
Then Lizzie weighed no more
Better and worse ;
But put a silver penny in her purse,
Kissed Laura, crossed the heath with clumps of furze
At twilight, halted by the brook :
And for the first time in her life
Began to listen and look.

Laughed every goblin
When they spied her peeping :
Came towards her hobbling,
Flying, running, leaping,
Puffing and blowing,
Chuckling, clapping, crowing,
Clucking and gobbling,
Mopping and mowing,

Full of airs and graces,
Pulling wry faces,
Demure grimaces,
Cat-like and rat-like,
Ratel- and wombat-like,
Snail-paced in a hurry,
Parrot-voiced and whistler,
Helter skelter, hurry skurry,
Chattering like magpies,
Fluttering like pigeons,
Gliding like fishes,—
Hugged her and kissed her :
Squeezed and caressed her :
Stretched up their dishes,
Panniers, and plates :
'Look at our apples
Russet and dun,
Bob at our cherries,
Bite at our peaches,
Citrons and dates,
Grapes for the asking,
Pears red with basking
Out in the sun,
Plums on their twigs ;
Pluck them and suck them,
Pomegranates, figs.'—

'Good folk,' said Lizzie,
Mindful of Jeanie :
'Give me much and many :'—

Held out her apron,
Tossed them her penny.
'Nay, take a seat with us,
Honour and eat with us,'
They answered grinning:
'Our feast is but beginning.
Night yet is early,
Warm and dew-pearly,
Wakeful and starry:
Such fruits as these
No man can carry;
Half their bloom would fly,
Half their dew would dry,
Half their flavour would pass by.
Sit down and feast with us,
Be welcome guest with us,
Cheer you and rest with us.'—
'Thank you,' said Lizzie: 'But one waits
At home alone for me:
So without further parleying,
If you will not sell me any
Of your fruits though much and many,
Give me back my silver penny
I tossed you for a fee.'—
They began to scratch their pates,
No longer wagging, purring,
But visibly demurring,
Grunting and snarling.
One called her proud,
Cross-grained, uncivil;

Their tones waxed loud,
Their looks were evil.
Lashing their tails
They trod and hustled her,
Elbowed and jostled her,
Clawed with their nails,
Barking, mewing, hissing, mocking,
Tore her gown and soiled her stocking,
Twitched her hair out by the roots,
Stamped upon her tender feet,
Held her hands and squeezed their fruits
Against her mouth to make her eat.

White and golden Lizzie stood,
Like a lily in a flood,—
Like a rock of blue-veined stone
Lashed by tides obstreperously,—
Like a beacon left alone
In a hoary roaring sea,
Sending up a golden fire,—
Like a fruit-crowned orange-tree
White with blossoms honey-sweet
Sore beset by wasp and bee,—
Like a royal virgin town
Topped with gilded dome and spire
Close beleaguered by a fleet
Mad to tug her standard down.

One may lead a horse to water,
Twenty cannot make him drink.

Though the goblins cuffed and caught her,
Coaxed and fought her,
Bullied and besought her,
Scratched her, pinched her black as ink,
Kicked and knocked her,
Mauled and mocked her,
Lizzie uttered not a word;
Would not open lip from lip
Lest they should cram a mouthful in:
But laughed in heart to feel the drip
Of juice that syrupped all her face,
And lodged in dimples of her chin,
And streaked her neck which quaked like curd.
At last the evil people
Worn out by her resistance
Flung back her penny, kicked their fruit
Along whichever road they took,
Not leaving root or stone or shoot;
Some writhed into the ground,
Some dived into the brook
With ring and ripple,
Some scudded on the gale without a sound,
Some vanished in the distance.

In a smart, ache, tingle,
Lizzie went her way;
Knew not was it night or day;
Sprang up the bank, tore thro' the furze,
Threaded copse and dingle,
And heard her penny jingle

Bouncing in her purse,—
Its bounce was music to her ear.
She ran and ran
As if she feared some goblin man
Dogged her with gibe or curse
Or something worse :
But not one goblin skurried after,
Nor was she pricked by fear ;
The kind heart made her windy-paced
That urged her home quite out of breath with haste
And inward laughter.

She cried 'Laura,' up the garden,
'Did you miss me ?
Come and kiss me.
Never mind my bruises,
Hug me, kiss me, suck my juices
Squeezed from goblin fruits for you,
Goblin pulp and goblin dew.
Eat me, drink me, love me ;
Laura, make much of me :
For your sake I have braved the glen
And had to do with goblin merchant men.'

Laura started from her chair,
Flung her arms up in the air,
Clutched her hair :
'Lizzie, Lizzie, have you tasted
For my sake the fruit forbidden ?
Must your light like mine be hidden,
Your young life like mine be wasted,

Undone in mine undoing
And ruined in my ruin,
Thirsty, cankered, goblin-ridden ?'—
She clung about her sister,
Kissed and kissed and kissed her:
Tears once again
Refreshed her shrunken eyes,
Dropping like rain
After long sultry drouth ;
Shaking with aguish fear, and pain,
She kissed and kissed her with a hungry mouth.

Her lips began to scorch,
That juice was wormwood to her tongue,
She loathed the feast:
Writhing as one possessed she leaped and sung,
Rent all her robe, and wrung
Her hands in lamentable haste,
And beat her breast.
Her locks streamed like the torch
Borne by a racer at full speed,
Or like the mane of horses in their flight,
Or like an eagle when she stems the light
Straight toward the sun,
Or like a caged thing freed,
Or like a flying flag when armies run.

Swift fire spread through her veins, knocked at her heart,
Met the fire smouldering there
And overbore its lesser flame ;

She gorged on bitterness without a name:
Ah! fool, to choose such part
Of soul-consuming care!
Sense failed in the mortal strife:
Like the watch-tower of a town
Which an earthquake shatters down,
Like a lightning-stricken mast,
Like a wind-uprooted tree
Spun about,
Like a foam-topped waterspout
Cast down headlong in the sea,
She fell at last;
Pleasure past and anguish past,
Is it death or is it life?

Life out of death.
That night long Lizzie watched by her,
Counted her pulse's flagging stir,
Felt for her breath,
Held water to her lips, and cooled her face
With tears and fanning leaves:
But when the first birds chirped about their eaves,
And early reapers plodded to the place
Of golden sheaves,
And dew-wet grass
Bowed in the morning winds so brisk to pass,
And new buds with new day
Opened of cup-like lilies on the stream,
Laura awoke as from a dream,
Laughed in the innocent old way,

Hugged Lizzie but not twice or thrice ;
Her gleaming locks showed not one thread of grey,
Her breath was sweet as May
And light danced in her eyes.

Days, weeks, months, years
Afterwards, when both were wives
With children of their own ;
Their mother-hearts beset with fears,
Their lives bound up in tender lives ;
Laura would call the little ones
And tell them of her early prime,
Those pleasant days long gone
Of not-returning time :
Would talk about the haunted glen,
The wicked, quaint fruit-merchant men,
Their fruits like honey to the throat
But poison in the blood ;
(Men sell not such in any town :)
Would tell them how her sister stood
In deadly peril to do her good,
And win the fiery antidote :
Then joining hands to little hands
Would bid them cling together,
'For there is no friend like a sister
In calm or stormy weather ;
To cheer one on the tedious way,
To fetch one if one goes astray,
To lift one if one totters down,
To strengthen whilst one stands.'

21

IN THE ROUND TOWER AT JHANSI

JUNE 8, 1857

A HUNDRED, a thousand to one ; even so ;
  Not a hope in the world remained :
The swarming howling wretches below
  Gained and gained and gained.

Skene looked at his pale young wife :—
  'Is the time come ?'—'The time is come !'—
Young, strong, and so full of life :
  The agony struck them dumb.

Close his arm about her now,
  Close her cheek to his,
Close the pistol to her brow—
  God forgive them this !

'Will it hurt much ?'—'No, mine own :
  I wish I could bear the pang for both.'
'I wish I could bear the pang alone :
  Courage, dear, I am not loth.'

Kiss and kiss : 'It is not pain
  Thus to kiss and die.
One kiss more.'—'And yet one again.'—
  'Good-bye.'—'Good-bye.'

DREAM LAND

WHERE sunless rivers weep
Their waves into the deep,
She sleeps a charmèd sleep :
  Awake her not.
Led by a single star,
She came from very far
To seek where shadows are
  Her pleasant lot.

She left the rosy morn,
She left the fields of corn,
For twilight cold and lorn
  And water springs.
Through sleep, as through a veil,
She sees the sky look pale,
And hears the nightingale
  That sadly sings.

Rest, rest, a perfect rest
Shed over brow and breast ;
Her face is toward the west,
  The purple land.
She cannot see the grain
Ripening on hill and plain ;
She cannot feel the rain
  Upon her hand.

Rest, rest, for evermore
Upon a mossy shore;
Rest, rest at the heart's core
Till time shall cease:
Sleep that no pain shall wake,
Night that no morn shall break
Till joy shall overtake
Her perfect peace.

AT HOME

When I was dead, my spirit turned
To seek the much-frequented house:
I passed the door, and saw my friends
Feasting beneath green orange boughs;
From hand to hand they pushed the wine,
They sucked the pulp of plum and peach;
They sang, they jested, and they laughed,
For each was loved of each.

I listened to their honest chat:
Said one: 'To-morrow we shall be
Plod plod along the featureless sands
And coasting miles and miles of sea.'
Said one: 'Before the turn of tide
We will achieve the eyrie-seat.'
Said one: 'To-morrow shall be like
To-day, but much more sweet.'

'To-morrow,' said they, strong with hope,
And dwelt upon the pleasant way:
'To-morrow,' cried they one and all,
While no one spoke of yesterday.
Their life stood full at blessed noon;
I, only I, had passed away:
'To-morrow and to-day,' they cried;
I was of yesterday.

I shivered comfortless, but cast
No chill across the tablecloth;
I all-forgotten shivered, sad
To stay and yet to part how loth:
I passed from the familiar room,
I who from love had passed away,
Like the remembrance of a guest
That tarrieth but a day.

A TRIAD

SONNET

THREE sang of love together: one with lips
Crimson, with cheeks and bosom in a glow,
Flushed to the yellow hair and finger-tips;
And one there sang who soft and smooth as snow
Bloomed like a tinted hyacinth at a show;
And one was blue with famine after love,
Who like a harpstring snapped rang harsh and low
The burden of what those were singing of.

One shamed herself in love ; one temperately
  Grew gross in soulless love, a sluggish wife ;
One famished died for love. Thus two of three
  Took death for love and won him after strife ;
One droned in sweetness like a fattened bee :
  All on the threshold, yet all short of life.

LOVE FROM THE NORTH

I HAD a love in soft south land,
  Beloved through April far in May ;
He waited on my lightest breath,
  And never dared to say me nay.

He saddened if my cheer was sad,
  But gay he grew if I was gay ;
We never differed on a hair,
  My yes his yes, my nay his nay.

The wedding hour was come, the aisles
  Were flushed with sun and flowers that day ;
I pacing balanced in my thoughts : 11
  ' It 's quite too late to think of nay.'—

My bridegroom answered in his turn,
  Myself had almost answered 'yea :'
When through the flashing nave I heard
  A struggle and resounding ' nay.'

Bridemaids and bridegroom shrank in fear,
But I stood high who stood at bay:
'And if I answer yea, fair Sir,
What man art thou to bar with nay?'

He was a strong man from the north,
Light-locked, with eyes of dangerous grey:
'Put yea by for another time
In which I will not say thee nay.'

He took me in his strong white arms,
He bore me on his horse away
O'er crag, morass, and hairbreadth pass,
But never asked me yea or nay.

He made me fast with book and bell,
With links of love he makes me stay;
Till now I've neither heart nor power
Nor will nor wish to say him nay.

WINTER RAIN

EVERY valley drinks,
Every dell and hollow:
Where the kind rain sinks and sinks,
Green of Spring will follow.

Yet a lapse of weeks
Buds will burst their edges,
Strip their wool-coats, glue-coats, streaks,
In the woods and hedges;

Weave a bower of love
  For birds to meet each other,
Weave a canopy above
  Nest and egg and mother.

But for fattening rain
  We should have no flowers,
Never a bud or leaf again
  But for soaking showers ;

Never a mated bird
  In the rocking tree-tops,
Never indeed a flock or herd
  To graze upon the lea-crops.

Lambs so woolly white,
  Sheep the sun-bright leas on,
They could have no grass to bite
  But for rain in season.

We should find no moss
  In the shadiest places,
Find no waving meadow grass
  Pied with broad-eyed daisies :

But miles of barren sand,
  With never a son or daughter,
Not a lily on the land,
  Or lily on the water.

COUSIN KATE

I WAS a cottage maiden
  Hardened by sun and air,
Contented with my cottage mates,
  Not mindful I was fair.
Why did a great lord find me out,
  And praise my flaxen hair ?
Why did a great lord find me out
  To fill my heart with care ?

He lured me to his palace home—
  Woe 's me for joy thereof—
To lead a shameless shameful life,
  His plaything and his love.
He wore me like a silken knot,
  He changed me like a glove ;
So now I moan, an unclean thing,
  Who might have been a dove.

O Lady Kate, my cousin Kate,
  You grew more fair than I :
He saw you at your father's gate,
  Chose you, and cast me by.
He watched your steps along the lane,
  Your work among the rye ;
He lifted you from mean estate
  To sit with him on high.

Because you were so good and pure
  He bound you with his ring :
The neighbours call you good and pure,
  Call me an outcast thing.
Even so I sit and howl in dust,
  You sit in gold and sing :
Now which of us has tenderer heart ?
  You had the stronger wing.

O cousin Kate, my love was true,
  Your love was writ in sand :
If he had fooled not me but you,
  If you stood where I stand,
He'd not have won me with his love
  Nor bought me with his land ;
I would have spit into his face
  And not have taken his hand.

Yet I've a gift you have not got,
  And seem not like to get :
For all your clothes and wedding-ring
  I've little doubt you fret.
My fair-haired son, my shame, my pride,
  Cling closer, closer yet :
Your father would give lands for one
  To wear his coronet.

NOBLE SISTERS

'Now did you mark a falcon,
  Sister dear, sister dear,
Flying toward my window
  In the morning cool and clear?
With jingling bells about her neck,
  But what beneath her wing?
It may have been a ribbon,
  Or it may have been a ring.'—
    'I marked a falcon swooping
      At the break of day:
    And for your love, my sister dove,
      I 'frayed the thief away.'—

'Or did you spy a ruddy hound,
  Sister fair and tall,
Went snuffing round my garden bound,
  Or crouched by my bower wall?
With a silken leash about his neck;
  But in his mouth may be
A chain of gold and silver links,
  Or a letter writ to me.'—
    'I heard a hound, highborn sister,
      Stood baying at the moon:
    I rose and drove him from your wall
      Lest you should wake too soon.'—

'Or did you meet a pretty page
Sat swinging on the gate;
Sat whistling whistling like a bird,
Or may be slept too late:
With eaglets broidered on his cap,
And eaglets on his glove?
If you had turned his pockets out,
You had found some pledge of love.'—
'I met him at this daybreak,
Scarce the east was red:
Lest the creaking gate should anger you,
I packed him home to bed.'—

'Oh patience, sister. Did you see
A young man tall and strong,
Swift-footed to uphold the right
And to uproot the wrong,
Come home across the desolate sea
To woo me for his wife?
And in his heart my heart is locked,
And in his life my life.'—
'I met a nameless man, sister,
Hard by your chamber door:
I said: Her husband loves her much.
And yet she loves him more.'—

'Fie, sister, fie, a wicked lie,
A lie, a wicked lie,
I have none other love but him,
Nor will have till I die.

And you have turned him from our door,
 And stabbed him with a lie :
I will go seek him thro' the world
 In sorrow till I die.'—
 ' Go seek in sorrow, sister,
 And find in sorrow too :
 If thus you shame our father's name
 My curse go forth with you.'

SPRING

FROST-LOCKED all the winter,
Seeds, and roots, and stones of fruits,
What shall make their sap ascend
That they may put forth shoots ?
Tips of tender green,
Leaf, or blade, or sheath ;
Telling of the hidden life
That breaks forth underneath,
Life nursed in its grave by Death.

Blows the thaw-wind pleasantly,
Drips the soaking rain,
By fits looks down the waking sun :
Young grass springs on the plain ;
Young leaves clothe early hedgerow trees ;
Seeds, and roots, and stones of fruits,
Swollen with sap put forth their shoots ;
Curled-headed ferns sprout in the lane ;
Birds sing and pair again.

There is no time like Spring,
When life 's alive in everything,
Before new nestlings sing,
Before cleft swallows speed their journey back
Along the trackless track—
God guides their wing,
He spreads their table that they nothing lack,—
Before the daisy grows a common flower,
Before the sun has power
To scorch the world up in his noontide hour.

There is no time like Spring,
Like Spring that passes by ;
There is no life like Spring-life born to die,—
Piercing the sod,
Clothing the uncouth clod,
Hatched in the nest,
Fledged on the windy bough,
Strong on the wing :
There is no time like Spring that passes by,
Now newly born, and now
Hastening to die.

THE LAMBS OF GRASMERE, 1860

The upland flocks grew starved and thinned:
 Their shepherds scarce could feed the lambs
Whose milkless mothers butted them,
 Or who were orphaned of their dams.
The lambs athirst for mother's milk
 Filled all the place with piteous sounds:
Their mothers' bones made white for miles
 The pastureless wet pasture grounds.

Day after day, night after night,
 From lamb to lamb the shepherds went,
With teapots for the bleating mouths
 Instead of nature's nourishment.
The little shivering gaping things
 Soon knew the step that brought them aid,
And fondled the protecting hand,
 And rubbed it with a woolly head.

Then, as the days waxed on to weeks,
 It was a pretty sight to see
These lambs with frisky heads and tails
 Skipping and leaping on the lea,
Bleating in tender, trustful tones,
 Resting on rocky crag or mound.
And following the beloved feet
 That once had sought for them and found.

These very shepherds of their flocks,
  These loving lambs so meek to please,
Are worthy of recording words
  And honour in their due degrees:
So I might live a hundred years,
  And roam from strand to foreign strand,
Yet not forget this flooded spring
  And scarce-saved lambs of Westmoreland.

A BIRTHDAY

My heart is like a singing bird
  Whose nest is in a watered shoot;
My heart is like an apple-tree
  Whose boughs are bent with thickset fruit;
My heart is like a rainbow shell
  That paddles in a halcyon sea;
My heart is gladder than all these
  Because my love is come to me.

Raise me a dais of silk and down;
  Hang it with vair and purple dyes;
Carve it in doves, and pomegranates,
  And peacocks with a hundred eyes;
Work it in gold and silver grapes,
  In leaves, and silver fleurs-de-lys;
Because the birthday of my life
  Is come, my love is come to me.

REMEMBER

SONNET

REMEMBER me when I am gone away,
  Gone far away into the silent land ;
  When you can no more hold me by the hand,
Nor I half turn to go yet turning stay.
Remember me when no more day by day
  You tell me of our future that you planned :
  Only remember me ; you understand
It will be late to counsel then or pray.
Yet if you should forget me for a while
  And afterwards remember, do not grieve :
  For if the darkness and corruption leave
  A vestige of the thoughts that once I had,
Better by far you should forget and smile
  Than that you should remember and be sad.

AFTER DEATH

SONNET

THE curtains were half drawn, the floor was swept
  And strewn with rushes, rosemary and may
  Lay thick upon the bed on which I lay,
Where through the lattice ivy-shadows crept.
He leaned above me, thinking that I slept
  And could not hear him ; but I heard him say :
  'Poor child, poor child :' and as he turned away
Came a deep silence, and I knew he wept.

He did not touch the shroud, or raise the fold
That hid my face, or take my hand in his,
Or ruffle the smooth pillows for my head:
He did not love me living; but once dead
He pitied me; and very sweet it is
To know he still is warm though I am cold.

AN END

Love, strong as Death, is dead.
Come, let us make his bed
Among the dying flowers:
A green turf at his head;
And a stone at his feet,
Whereon we may sit
In the quiet evening hours.

He was born in the Spring,
And died before the harvesting:
On the last warm summer day
He left us; he would not stay
For Autumn twilight cold and grey.
Sit we by his grave, and sing
He is gone away.

To few chords and sad and low
Sing we so:
Be our eyes fixed on the grass
Shadow-veiled as the years pass
While we think of all that was
In the long ago.

MY DREAM

HEAR now a curious dream I dreamed last night
Each word whereof is weighed and sifted truth.

I stood beside Euphrates while it swelled
Like overflowing Jordan in its youth:
It waxed and coloured sensibly to sight;
Till out of myriad pregnant waves there welled
Young crocodiles, a gaunt blunt-featured crew,
Fresh-hatched perhaps and daubed with birthday dew.
The rest if I should tell, I fear my friend
My closest friend would deem the facts untrue;
And therefore it were wisely left untold;
Yet if you will, why, hear it to the end.

Each crocodile was girt with massive gold
And polished stones that with their wearers grew:
But one there was who waxed beyond the rest,
Wore kinglier girdle and a kingly crown,
Whilst crowns and orbs and sceptres starred his breast.
All gleamed compact and green with scale on scale,
But special burnishment adorned his mail
And special terror weighed upon his frown;
His punier brethren quaked before his tail,
Broad as a rafter, potent as a flail.

So he grew lord and master of his kin:
But who shall tell the tale of all their woes?
An execrable appetite arose,
He battened on them, crunched, and sucked them in.
He knew no law, he feared no binding law,
But ground them with inexorable jaw:
The luscious fat distilled upon his chin,
Exuded from his nostrils and his eyes,
While still like hungry death he fed his maw;
Till every minor crocodile being dead
And buried too, himself gorged to the full,
He slept with breath oppressed and unstrung claw.
Oh marvel passing strange which next I saw:
In sleep he dwindled to the common size,
And all the empire faded from his coat.
Then from far off a wingèd vessel came,
Swift as a swallow, subtle as a flame:
I know not what it bore of freight or host,
But white it was as an avenging ghost.
It levelled strong Euphrates in its course;
Supreme yet weightless as an idle mote
It seemed to tame the waters without force
Till not a murmur swelled or billow beat:
Lo, as the purple shadow swept the sands,
The prudent crocodile rose on his feet
And shed appropriate tears and wrung his hands.

What can it mean? you ask. I answer not
For meaning, but myself must echo, What?
And tell it as I saw it on the spot.

SONG

Oh roses for the flush of youth,
  And laurel for the perfect prime;
But pluck an ivy branch for me
  Grown old before my time.

Oh violets for the grave of youth,
  And bay for those dead in their prime;
Give me the withered leaves I chose
  Before in the old time.

THE HOUR AND THE GHOST

BRIDE

O love, love, hold me fast,
He draws me away from thee;
I cannot stem the blast,
Nor the cold strong sea:
Far away a light shines
Beyond the hills and pines;
It is lit for me.

BRIDEGROOM

I have thee close, my dear,
No terror can come near;
Only far off the northern light shines clear.

GHOST

Come with me, fair and false,
To our home, come home.
It is my voice that calls :
Once thou wast not afraid
When I woo'd, and said,
'Come, our nest is newly made'—
Now cross the tossing foam.

BRIDE

Hold me one moment longer,
He taunts me with the past,
His clutch is waxing stronger,
Hold me fast, hold me fast.
He draws me from thy heart,
And I cannot withhold :
He bids my spirit depart
With him into the cold :—
Oh bitter vows of old !

BRIDEGROOM

Lean on me, hide thine eyes :
Only ourselves, earth and skies,
Are present here : be wise.

GHOST

Lean on me, come away,
I will guide and steady :
Come, for I will not stay :
Come, for house and bed are ready.

Ah, sure bed and house,
For better and worse, for life and death :
Goal won with shortened breath :
Come, crown our vows.

BRIDE

One moment, one more word,
While my heart beats still,
While my breath is stirred
By my fainting will.
O friend forsake me not,
Forget not as I forgot :
But keep thy heart for me,
Keep thy faith true and bright ;
Through the lone cold winter night
Perhaps I may come to thee.

BRIDEGROOM

Nay peace, my darling, peace :
Let these dreams and terrors cease :
Who spoke of death or change or aught but ease ?

GHOST

O fair frail sin,
O poor harvest gathered in !
Thou shalt visit him again
To watch his heart grow cold ;
To know the gnawing pain
I knew of old ;
To see one much more fair

Fill up the vacant chair,
Fill his heart, his children bear :—
While thou and I together
In the outcast weather
Toss and howl and spin.

A SUMMER WISH

LIVE all thy sweet life thro',
  Sweet Rose, dew-sprent,
Drop down thine evening dew
To gather it anew
When day is bright :
  I fancy thou wast meant
Chiefly to give delight.

Sing in the silent sky,
  Glad soaring bird ;
Sing out thy notes on high
To sunbeam straying by
Or passing cloud ;
  Heedless if thou art heard
Sing thy full song aloud.

Oh that it were with me
  As with the flower ;
Blooming on its own tree
For butterfly and bee
Its summer morns :
  That I might bloom mine hour
A rose in spite of thorns.

Oh that my work were done
  As birds' that soar
Rejoicing in the sun :
That when my time is run
And daylight too,
  I so might rest once more
Cool with refreshing dew. 28

AN APPLE GATHERING

I PLUCKED pink blossoms from mine apple-tree
  And wore them all that evening in my hair :
Then in due season when I went to see
    I found no apples there.

With dangling basket all along the grass
  As I had come I went the selfsame track :
My neighbours mocked me while they saw me pass
    So empty-handed back.

Lilian and Lilias smiled in trudging by, 9
  Their heaped-up basket teased me like a jeer ;
Sweet-voiced they sang beneath the sunset sky,
    Their mother's home was near.

Plump Gertrude passed me with her basket full,
  A stronger hand than hers helped it along ;
A voice talked with her through the shadows cool
    More sweet to me than song.

Ah Willie, Willie, was my love less worth
  Than apples with their green leaves piled above ?
I counted rosiest apples on the earth
  Of far less worth than love.

So once it was with me you stooped to talk
  Laughing and listening in this very lane :
To think that by this way we used to walk
  We shall not walk again !

I let my neighbours pass me, ones and twos
  And groups ; the latest said the night grew chill,
And hastened : but I loitered, while the dews
  Fell fast I loitered still.

SONG

Two doves upon the selfsame branch,
  Two lilies on a single stem,
Two butterflies upon one flower :—
  Oh happy they who look on them.

Who look upon them hand in hand
  Flushed in the rosy summer light ;
Who look upon them hand in hand
  And never give a thought to night.

MAUDE CLARE

OUT of the church she followed them
  With a lofty step and mien :
His bride was like a village maid,
  Maude Clare was like a queen.

'Son Thomas,' his lady mother said,
  With smiles, almost with tears :
'May Nell and you but live as true
  As we have done for years ;

'Your father thirty years ago
  Had just your tale to tell ;
But he was not so pale as you,
  Nor I so pale as Nell.'

My lord was pale with inward strife,
  And Nell was pale with pride ;
My lord gazed long on pale Maude Clare
  Or ever he kissed the bride.

'Lo, I have brought my gift, my lord,
  Have brought my gift,' she said :
'To bless the hearth, to bless the board,
  To bless the marriage-bed.

'Here 's my half of the golden chain
  You wore about your neck,
That day we waded ankle-deep
  For lilies in the beck :

'Here 's my half of the faded leaves
  We plucked from budding bough,
With feet amongst the lily leaves,—
  The lilies are budding now.'

He strove to match her scorn with scorn,
  He faltered in his place :
'Lady,' he said,—'Maude Clare,' he said,—
  'Maude Clare : '—and hid his face.

She turn'd to Nell : 'My Lady Nell,
  I have a gift for you ;
Though, were it fruit, the bloom were gone,
  Or, were it flowers, the dew.

'Take my share of a fickle heart,
  Mine of a paltry love :
Take it or leave it as you will,
  I wash my hands thereof.'

'And what you leave,' said Nell, 'I'll take,
  And what you spurn, I'll wear ;
For he 's my lord for better and worse,
  And him I love, Maude Clare.

'Yea, though you're taller by the head,
  More wise, and much more fair ;
I'll love him till he loves me best,
  Me best of all, Maude Clare.'

ECHO

Come to me in the silence of the night;
Come in the speaking silence of a dream;
Come with soft rounded cheeks and eyes as bright
As sunlight on a stream;
Come back in tears,
O memory, hope, love of finished years.

Oh dream how sweet, too sweet, too bitter sweet,
Whose wakening should have been in Paradise,
Where souls brimfull of love abide and meet;
Where thirsting longing eyes
Watch the slow door
That opening, letting in, lets out no more.

Yet come to me in dreams, that I may live
My very life again though cold in death:
Come back to me in dreams, that I may give
Pulse for pulse, breath for breath:
Speak low, lean low,
As long ago, my love, how long ago!

MY SECRET

I tell my secret? No indeed, not I:
Perhaps some day, who knows?
But not to-day; it froze, and blows, and snows,
And you're too curious: fie!
You want to hear it? well:
Only, my secret 's mine, and I won't tell.

Or, after all, perhaps there's none:
Suppose there is no secret after all,
But only just my fun.
To-day's a nipping day, a biting day;
In which one wants a shawl,
A veil, a cloak, and other wraps:
I cannot ope to every one who taps,
And let the draughts come whistling through my
hall;
Come bounding and surrounding me,
Come buffeting, astounding me,
Nipping and clipping through my wraps and all.
I wear my mask for warmth: who ever shows
His nose to Russian snows
To be pecked at by every wind that blows?
You would not peck? I thank you for good will,
Believe, but leave that truth untested still.

Spring's an expansive time: yet I don't trust
March with its peck of dust,
Nor April with its rainbow-crowned brief showers,
Nor even May, whose flowers
One frost may wither through the sunless hours.

Perhaps some languid summer day,
When drowsy birds sing less and less,
And golden fruit is ripening to excess,
If there's not too much sun nor too much cloud,
And the warm wind is neither still nor loud,
Perhaps my secret I may say,
Or you may guess.

ANOTHER SPRING

If I might see another Spring
I'd not plant summer flowers and wait:
I'd have my crocuses at once,
My leafless pink mezereons,
My chill-veined snowdrops, choicer yet
My white or azure violet,
Leaf-nested primrose; anything
To blow at once not late.

If I might see another Spring
I'd listen to the daylight birds
That build their nests and pair and sing,
Nor wait for mateless nightingale;
I'd listen to the lusty herds,
The ewes with lambs as white as snow,
I'd find out music in the hail
And all the winds that blow.

If I might see another Spring—
Oh stinging comment on my past
That all my past results in 'if'—
If I might see another Spring
I'd laugh to-day, to-day is brief;
I would not wait for anything:
I'd use to-day that cannot last,
Be glad to-day and sing.

A PEAL OF BELLS

STRIKE the bells wantonly,
  Tinkle tinkle well;
Bring me wine, bring me flowers,
  Ring the silver bell.
All my lamps burn scented oil,
  Hung on laden orange-trees,
Whose shadowed foliage is the foil
  To golden lamps and oranges.
Heap my golden plates with fruit,
  Golden fruit, fresh-plucked and ripe;
  Strike the bells and breathe the pipe;
Shut out showers from summer hours—
Silence that complaining lute—
  Shut out thinking, shut out pain,
  From hours that cannot come again.

Strike the bells solemnly,
  Ding dong deep:
My friend is passing to his bed,
  Fast asleep;
There's plaited linen round his head,
  While foremost go his feet—
His feet that cannot carry him
My feast's a show, my lights are dim;
  Be still, your music is not sweet,—
There is no music more for him:

His lights are out, his feast is done ;
His bowl that sparkled to the brim
Is drained, is broken, cannot hold ;
My blood is chill, his blood is cold ;
His death is full, and mine begun.

FATA MORGANA

A BLUE-EYED phantom far before
Is laughing, leaping toward the sun :
Like lead I chase it evermore,
I pant and run.

It breaks the sunlight bound on bound :
Goes singing as it leaps along
To sheep-bells with a dreamy sound
A dreamy song.

I laugh, it is so brisk and gay ;
It is so far before, I weep :
I hope I shall lie down some day,
Lie down and sleep.

'NO, THANK YOU, JOHN'

I NEVER said I loved you, John :
Why will you tease me day by day,
And wax a weariness to think upon
With always 'do' and 'pray' ?

You know I never loved you, John;
  No fault of mine made me your toast:
Why will you haunt me with a face as wan
    As shows an hour-old ghost?

I dare say Meg or Moll would take
  Pity upon you, if you'd ask:
And pray don't remain single for my sake
    Who can't perform that task.

I have no heart?—Perhaps I have not;
  But then you're mad to take offence
That I don't give you what I have not got:
    Use your own common sense.

Let bygones be bygones:
  Don't call me false, who owed not to be true:
I'd rather answer 'No' to fifty Johns
    Than answer 'Yes' to you.

Let's mar our pleasant days no more,
  Song-birds of passage, days of youth:
Catch at to-day, forget the days before:
    I'll wink at your untruth.

Let us strike hands as hearty friends;
  No more, no less; and friendship's good:
Only don't keep in view ulterior ends,
    And points not understood

In open treaty. Rise above
  Quibbles and shuffling off and on:
Here's friendship for you if you like; but love,—
    No, thank you, John.

MAY

I CANNOT tell you how it was;
But this I know: it came to pass
Upon a bright and breezy day
When May was young; ah, pleasant May!
As yet the poppies were not born
Between the blades of tender corn;
The last eggs had not hatched as yet,
Nor any bird forgone its mate.

I cannot tell you what it was;
But this I know: it did but pass.
It passed away with sunny May,
With all sweet things it passed away,
And left me old, and cold, and grey.

A PAUSE OF THOUGHT

I LOOKED for that which is not, nor can be,
And hope deferred made my heart sick in truth:
But years must pass before a hope of youth
Is resigned utterly.

I watched and waited with a steadfast will:
And though the object seemed to flee away
That I so longed for, ever day by day
I watched and waited still.

Sometimes I said : This thing shall be no more ;
My expectation wearies and shall cease ;
I will resign it now and be at peace :
Yet never gave it o'er.

Sometimes I said : It is an empty name
I long for ; to a name why should I give
The peace of all the days I have to live ?—
Yet gave it all the same.

Alas, thou foolish one ! alike unfit
For healthy joy and salutary pain :
Thou knowest the chase useless, and again
Turnest to follow it.

TWILIGHT CALM

Oh, pleasant eventide !
Clouds on the western side
Grow grey and greyer hiding the warm sun :
The bees and birds, their happy labours done,
Seek their close nests and bide.

Screened in the leafy wood
The stock-doves sit and brood :
The very squirrel leaps from bough to bough
But lazily ; pauses ; and settles now
Where once he stored his food.

One by one the flowers close,
Lily and dewy rose
Shutting their tender petals from the moon:
The grasshoppers are still; but not so soon
Are still the noisy crows.

The dormouse squats and eats
Choice little dainty bits
Beneath the spreading roots of a broad lime;
Nibbling his fill he stops from time to time
And listens where he sits.

From far the lowings come
Of cattle driven home:
From farther still the wind brings fitfully
The vast continual murmur of the sea,
Now loud, now almost dumb.

The gnats whirl in the air,
The evening gnats; and there
The owl opes broad his eyes and wings to sail
For prey; the bat wakes; and the shell-less snail
Comes forth, clammy and bare.

Hark! that's the nightingale,
Telling the selfsame tale
Her song told when this ancient earth was young:
So echoes answered when her song was sung
In the first wooded vale.

We call it love and pain
The passion of her strain ;
And yet we little understand or know :
Why should it not be rather joy that so
Throbs in each throbbing vein ?

In separate herds the deer
Lie ; here the bucks, and here
The does, and by its mother sleeps the fawn :
Through all the hours of night until the dawn
They sleep, forgetting fear.

The hare sleeps where it lies,
With wary half-closed eyes ;
The cock has ceased to crow, the hen to cluck :
Only the fox is out, some heedless duck
Or chicken to surprise.

Remote, each single star
Comes out, till there they are
All shining brightly : how the dews fall damp !
While close at hand the glow-worm lights her lamp
Or twinkles from afar.

But evening now is done
As much as if the sun
Day-giving had arisen in the East :
For night has come ; and the great calm has ceased,
The quiet sands have run.

WIFE TO HUSBAND

Pardon the faults in me,
For the love of years ago:
Good-bye.
I must drift across the sea,
I must sink into the snow,
I must die.

You can bask in this sun,
You can drink wine, and eat:
Good-bye.
I must gird myself and run,
Though with unready feet:
I must die.

Blank sea to sail upon,
Cold bed to sleep in:
Good-bye.
While you clasp, I must be gone
For all your weeping:
I must die.

A kiss for one friend,
And a word for two,—
Good-bye:—
A lock that you must send,
A kindness you must do:
I must die.

Not a word for you,
Not a lock or kiss,
Good-bye.
We, one, must part in two;
Verily death is this:
I must die.

THREE SEASONS

‘A cup for hope!’ she said,
In springtime ere the bloom was old:
The crimson wine was poor and cold
By her mouth's richer red.

‘A cup for love!’ how low,
How soft the words; and all the while
Her blush was rippling with a smile
Like summer after snow.

‘A cup for memory!’
Cold cup that one must drain alone:
While autumn winds are up and moan
Across the barren sea.

Hope, memory, love:
Hope for fair morn, and love for day,
And memory for the evening grey
And solitary dove.

MIRAGE

THE hope I dreamed of was a dream,
  Was but a dream; and now I wake
Exceeding comfortless, and worn, and old,
  For a dream's sake.

I hang my harp upon a tree,
  A weeping willow in a lake;
I hang my silenced harp there, wrung and snapt
  For a dream's sake.

Lie still, lie still, my breaking heart;
  My silent heart, lie still and break:
Life, and the world, and mine own self, are changed
  For a dream's sake.

SHUT OUT

THE door was shut. I looked between
  Its iron bars; and saw it lie,
  My garden, mine, beneath the sky,
Pied with all flowers bedewed and green:

From bough to bough the song-birds crossed,
  From flower to flower the moths and bees;
  With all its nests and stately trees
It had been mine, and it was lost.

A shadowless spirit kept the gate,
Blank and unchanging like the grave.
I peering through said: 'Let me have
Some buds to cheer my outcast state.'

He answered not. 'Or give me, then,
But one small twig from shrub or tree;
And bid my home remember me
Until I come to it again.'

The spirit was silent; but he took
Mortar and stone to build a wall;
He left no loophole great or small
Through which my straining eyes might look:

So now I sit here quite alone
Blinded with tears; nor grieve for that,
For nought is left worth looking at
Since my delightful land is gone.

A violet bed is budding near,
Wherein a lark has made her nest:
And good they are, but not the best;
And dear they are, but not so dear.

SOUND SLEEP

Some are laughing, some are weeping;
She is sleeping, only sleeping.
Round her rest wild flowers are creeping;
There the wind is heaping, heaping
Sweetest sweets of Summer's keeping.
By the corn-fields ripe for reaping.

There are lilies, and there blushes
The deep rose, and there the thrushes
Sing till latest sunlight flushes
In the west; a fresh wind brushes
Through the leaves while evening hushes.

There by day the lark is singing
And the grass and weeds are springing;
There by night the bat is winging;
There for ever winds are bringing
Far-off chimes of church-bells ringing.

Night and morning, noon and even,
Their sound fills her dreams with Heaven:
The long strife at length is striven:
Till her grave-bands shall be riven
Such is the good portion given
To her soul at rest and shriven.

SONG

SHE sat and sang alway
By the green margin of a stream,
Watching the fishes leap and play
Beneath the glad sunbeam.

I sat and wept alway
Beneath the moon's most shadowy beam,
Watching the blossoms of the May
Weep leaves into the stream.

I wept for memory;
She sang for hope that is so fair:
My tears were swallowed by the sea;
Her songs died on the air.

SONG

WHEN I am dead, my dearest,
Sing no sad songs for me;
Plant thou no roses at my head,
Nor shady cypress tree:
Be the green grass above me
With showers and dewdrops wet;
And if thou wilt, remember,
And if thou wilt, forget.

I shall not see the shadows,
  I shall not feel the rain ;
I shall not hear the nightingale
  Sing on, as if in pain :
And dreaming through the twilight
  That doth not rise nor set,
Haply I may remember,
  And haply may forget.

DEAD BEFORE DEATH

SONNET

AH ! changed and cold, how changed and very cold,
  With stiffened smiling lips and cold calm eyes :
  Changed, yet the same ; much knowing, little wise ;
This was the promise of the days of old !
Grown hard and stubborn in the ancient mould,
  Grown rigid in the sham of lifelong lies :
  We hoped for better things as years would rise,
But it is over as a tale once told.
All fallen the blossom that no fruitage bore,
  All lost the present and the future time,
All lost, all lost, the lapse that went before :
So lost till death shut-to the opened door,
  So lost from chime to everlasting chime,
So cold and lost for ever evermore.

BITTER FOR SWEET

SUMMER is gone with all its roses,
Its sun and perfumes and sweet flowers,
Its warm air and refreshing showers:
And even Autumn closes.

Yea, Autumn's chilly self is going,
And winter comes which is yet colder;
Each day the hoar-frost waxes bolder
And the last buds cease blowing.

SISTER MAUDE

WHO told my mother of my shame,
Who told my father of my dear?
Oh who but Maude, my sister Maude,
Who lurked to spy and peer.

Cold he lies, as cold as stone,
With his clotted curls about his face:
The comeliest corpse in all the world
And worthy of a queen's embrace.

You might have spared his soul, sister,
Have spared my soul, your own soul too:
Though I had not been born at all, 11
He'd never have looked at you.

My father may sleep in Paradise,
  My mother at Heaven-gate:
But sister Maude shall get no sleep
  Either early or late.

My father may wear a golden gown,
  My mother a crown may win;
If my dear and I knocked at Heaven-gate
  Perhaps they'd let us in:
But sister Maude, oh sister Maude,
  Bide *you* with death and sin.

REST

SONNET

O EARTH, lie heavily upon her eyes;
  Seal her sweet eyes weary of watching, Earth;
  Lie close around her; leave no room for mirth
With its harsh laughter, nor for sound of sighs.
She hath no questions, she hath no replies,
  Hushed in and curtained with a blessèd dearth
  Of all that irked her from the hour of birth;
With stillness that is almost Paradise.
Darkness more clear than noon-day holdeth her,
  Silence more musical than any song;
Even her very heart has ceased to stir:
Until the morning of Eternity
Her rest shall not begin nor end, but be;
  And when she wakes she will not think it long.

THE FIRST SPRING DAY

I WONDER if the sap is stirring yet,
If wintry birds are dreaming of a mate,
If frozen snowdrops feel as yet the sun
And crocus fires are kindling one by one:
    Sing, robin, sing;
I still am sore in doubt concerning Spring.

I wonder if the springtide of this year
Will bring another Spring both lost and dear;
If heart and spirit will find out their Spring,
Or if the world alone will bud and sing:
    Sing, hope, to me;
Sweet notes, my hope, soft notes for memory.

The sap will surely quicken soon or late,
The tardiest bird will twitter to a mate;
So Spring must dawn again with warmth and bloom,
Or in this world, or in the world to come:
    Sing, voice of Spring,
Till I too blossom and rejoice and sing.

THE CONVENT THRESHOLD

THERE'S blood between us, love, my love,
There's father's blood, there's brother's blood;
And blood's a bar I cannot pass:
I choose the stairs that mount above,
Stair after golden skyward stair,
To city and to sea of glass.

My lily feet are soiled with mud,
With scarlet mud which tells a tale
Of hope that was, of guilt that was,
Of love that shall not yet avail;
Alas, my heart, if I could bare
My heart, this selfsame stain is there:
I seek the sea of glass and fire
To wash the spot, to burn the snare;
Lo, stairs are meant to lift us higher:
Mount with me, mount the kindled stair.

Your eyes look earthward, mine look up.
I see the far-off city grand,
Beyond the hills a watered land,
Beyond the gulf a gleaming strand
Of mansions where the righteous sup;
Who sleep at ease among their trees,
Or wake to sing a cadenced hymn
With Cherubim and Seraphim;
They bore the Cross, they drained the cup,
Racked, roasted, crushed, wrenched limb from limb,
They the offscouring of the world:
The heaven of starry heavens unfurled,
The sun before their face is dim.

You looking earthward what see you?
Milk-white wine-flushed among the vines,
Up and down leaping, to and fro,
Most glad, most full, made strong with wines,
Blooming as peaches pearled with dew,

Their golden windy hair afloat,
Love-music warbling in their throat,
Young men and women come and go.

You linger, yet the time is short :
Flee for your life, gird up your strength
To flee ; the shadows stretched at length
Show that day wanes, that night draws nigh ;
Flee to the mountain, tarry not.
Is this a time for smile and sigh,
For songs among the secret trees
Where sudden blue birds nest and sport ?
The time is short and yet you stay :
To-day while it is called to-day
Kneel, wrestle, knock, do violence, pray ;
To-day is short, to-morrow nigh :
Why will you die ? why will you die ?

You sinned with me a pleasant sin :
Repent with me, for I repent.
Woe's me the lore I must unlearn !
Woe's me that easy way we went,
So rugged when I would return !
How long until my sleep begin,
How long shall stretch these nights and days ?
Surely, clean Angels cry, she prays ;
She laves her soul with tedious tears :
How long must stretch these years and years ?

I turn from you my cheeks and eyes,
My hair which you shall see no more—

Alas for joy that went before,
For joy that dies, for love that dies.
Only my lips still turn to you,
My livid lips that cry, Repent.
Oh weary life, oh weary Lent,
Oh weary time whose stars are few.

How should I rest in Paradise,
Or sit on steps of heaven alone ?
If Saints and Angels spoke of love
Should I not answer from my throne :
Have pity upon me, ye my friends,
For I have heard the sound thereof :
Should I not turn with yearning eyes,
Turn earthwards with a pitiful pang ?
Oh save me from a pang in heaven.
By all the gifts we took and gave,
Repent, repent, and be forgiven :
This life is long, but yet it ends ;
Repent and purge your soul and save :
No gladder song the morning stars
Upon their birthday morning sang
Than Angels sing when one repents.

I tell you what I dreamed last night :
A spirit with transfigured face
Fire-footed clomb an infinite space.
I heard his hundred pinions clang,
Heaven-bells rejoicing rang and rang,
Heaven-air was thrilled with subtle scents,

Worlds spun upon their rushing cars:
He mounted shrieking: 'Give me light.'
Still light was poured on him, more light;
Angels, Archangels he outstripped
Exultant in exceeding might,
And trod the skirts of Cherubim.
Still 'Give me light,' he shrieked; and dipped
His thirsty face, and drank a sea,
Athirst with thirst it could not slake.
I saw him, drunk with knowledge, take
From aching brows the aureole crown—
His locks writhed like a cloven snake—
He left his throne to grovel down
And lick the dust of Seraphs' feet:
For what is knowledge duly weighed?
Knowledge is strong, but love is sweet;
Yea all the progress he had made
Was but to learn that all is small
Save love, for love is all in all.

I tell you what I dreamed last night:
It was not dark, it was not light,
Cold dews had drenched my plenteous hair
Through clay; you came to seek me there.
And 'Do you dream of me?' you said.
My heart was dust that used to leap
To you; I answered half asleep:
'My pillow is damp, my sheets are red,
There's a leaden tester to my bed:
Find you a warmer playfellow,

A warmer pillow for your head,
A kinder love to love than mine.'
You wrung your hands; while I like lead
Crushed downwards through the sodden earth:
You smote your hands but not in mirth,
And reeled but were not drunk with wine.

For all night long I dreamed of you:
I woke and prayed against my will,
Then slept to dream of you again.
At length I rose and knelt and prayed:
I cannot write the words I said,
My words were slow, my tears were few;
But through the dark my silence spoke
Like thunder. When this morning broke,
My face was pinched, my hair was grey,
And frozen blood was on the sill
Where stifling in my struggle I lay.

If now you saw me you would say:
Where is the face I used to love?
And I would answer: Gone before;
It tarries veiled in paradise.
When once the morning star shall rise,
When earth with shadow flees away
And we stand safe within the door,
Then you shall lift the veil thereof.
Look up, rise up: for far above
Our palms are grown, our place is set;
There we shall meet as once we met
And love with old familiar love.

UP-HILL

DOES the road wind up-hill all the way?
  Yes, to the very end.
Will the day's journey take the whole long day?
  From morn to night, my friend.

But is there for the night a resting-place?
  A roof for when the slow dark hours begin.
May not the darkness hide it from my face?
  You cannot miss that inn.

Shall I meet other wayfarers at night?
  Those who have gone before.
Then must I knock, or call when just in sight?
  They will not keep you standing at that door.

Shall I find comfort, travel-sore and weak?
  Of labour you shall find the sum.
Will there be beds for me and all who seek?
  Yea, beds for all who come.

DEVOTIONAL PIECES

'THE LOVE OF CHRIST WHICH PASSETH KNOWLEDGE'

I bore with thee long weary days and nights,
Through many pangs of heart, through many tears ;
I bore with thee, thy hardness, coldness, slights,
For three and thirty years.

Who else had dared for thee what I have dared ?
I plunged the depth most deep from bliss above ;
I not My flesh, I not My spirit spared :
Give thou Me love for love.

For thee I thirsted in the daily drouth,
For thee I trembled in the nightly frost :
Much sweeter thou than honey to My mouth :
Why wilt thou still be lost ?

I bore thee on My shoulders and rejoiced :
Men only marked upon My shoulders borne
The branding cross ; and shouted hungry-voiced,
Or wagged their heads in scorn.

Thee did nails grave upon My hands, thy name
Did thorns for frontlets stamp between Mine eyes:
I, Holy One, put on thy guilt and shame;
I, God, Priest, Sacrifice.

A thief upon My right hand and My left;
Six hours alone, athirst, in misery:
At length in death one smote My heart and cleft
A hiding-place for thee.

Nailed to the racking cross, than bed of down
More dear, whereon to stretch Myself and sleep:
So did I win a kingdom,—share My crown;
A harvest,—come and reap.

'A BRUISED REED SHALL HE NOT BREAK'

I WILL accept thy will to do and be,
Thy hatred and intolerance of sin,
Thy will at least to love, that burns within
And thirsteth after Me:
So will I render fruitful, blessing still,
The germs and small beginnings in thy heart,
Because thy will cleaves to the better part.—
Alas, I cannot will.

Dost not thou will, poor soul? Yet I receive
The inner unseen longings of the soul,
I guide them turning towards Me; I control
And charm hearts till they grieve:

If thou desire, it yet shall come to pass,
  Though thou but wish indeed to choose My love ;
  For I have power in earth and heaven above.—
    I cannot wish, alas !

What, neither choose nor wish to choose ? and yet
  I still must strive to win thee and constrain :
  For thee I hung upon the cross in pain,
    How then can I forget ?
If thou as yet dost neither love, nor hate,
  Nor choose, nor wish,—resign thyself, be still
  Till I infuse love, hatred, longing, will.—
    I do not deprecate.

A BETTER RESURRECTION

I HAVE no wit, no words, no tears ;
  My heart within me like a stone
Is numbed too much for hopes or fears ;
  Look right, look left, I dwell alone ;
I lift mine eyes, but dimmed with grief
  No everlasting hills I see ;
My life is in the falling leaf :
    O Jesus, quicken me.

My life is like a faded leaf,
  My harvest dwindled to a husk ;
Truly my life is void and brief
  And tedious in the barren dusk ;

My life is like a frozen thing,
No bud nor greenness can I see:
Yet rise it shall—the sap of Spring;
O Jesus, rise in me.

My life is like a broken bowl,
A broken bowl that cannot hold
One drop of water for my soul
Or cordial in the searching cold;
Cast in the fire the perished thing,
Melt and remould it, till it be
A royal cup for Him my King:
O Jesus, drink of me.

ADVENT

THIS Advent moon shines cold and clear,
These Advent nights are long;
Our lamps have burned year after year
And still their flame is strong.
'Watchman, what of the night?' we cry,
Heart-sick with hope deferred:
'No speaking signs are in the sky,'
Is still the watchman's word.

The Porter watches at the gate,
The servants watch within;
The watch is long betimes and late,
The prize is slow to win.

'Watchman, what of the night?' But still
His answer sounds the same:
'No daybreak tops the utmost hill,
Nor pale our lamps of flame.'

One to another hear them speak
The patient virgins wise:
'Surely He is not far to seek'—
'All night we watch and rise.'
'The days are evil looking back,
The coming days are dim;
Yet count we not His promise slack,
But watch and wait for Him.'

One with another, soul with soul,
They kindle fire from fire:
'Friends watch us who have touched the goal.'
'They urge us, come up higher.'
'With them shall rest our waysore feet,
With them is built our home,
With Christ.'—'They sweet, but He most sweet,
Sweeter than honeycomb.'

There no more parting, no more pain,
The distant ones brought near,
The lost so long are found again,
Long lost but longer dear:
Eye hath not seen, ear hath not heard,
Nor heart conceived that rest,
With them our good things long deferred,
With Jesus Christ our Best.

We weep because the night is long,
  We laugh for day shall rise,
We sing a slow contented song
  And knock at Paradise.
Weeping we hold Him fast, Who wept
  For us, we hold Him fast ;
And will not let Him go except
  He bless us first or last.

Weeping we hold Him fast to-night ;
  We will not let Him go
Till daybreak smite our wearied sight
  And summer smite the snow :
Then figs shall bud, and dove with dove
  Shall coo the livelong day ;
Then He shall say, 'Arise, My love,
  My fair one, come away.'

THE THREE ENEMIES

THE FLESH

'Sweet, thou art pale.'
                    'More pale to see,
Christ hung upon the cruel tree
And bore His Father's wrath for me.'

'Sweet, thou art sad.'
                    'Beneath a rod
More heavy, Christ for my sake trod
The winepress of the wrath of God.'

'Sweet, thou art weary.'
'Not so Christ:
Whose mighty love of me sufficed
For Strength, Salvation, Eucharist.'

'Sweet, thou art footsore.'
'If I bleed,
His feet have bled: yea, in my need
His Heart once bled for mine indeed.'

THE WORLD

'Sweet, thou art young.'
'So He was young
Who for my sake in silence hung
Upon the Cross with Passion wrung.'

'Look, thou art fair.'
'He was more fair
Than men, Who deigned for me to wear
A visage marred beyond compare.'

'And thou hast riches.'
'Daily bread:
All else is His; Who living, dead,
For me lacked where to lay His Head.'

'And life is sweet.'
'It was not so
To Him, Whose Cup did overflow
With mine unutterable woe.'

THE DEVIL

'Thou drinkest deep.'
'When Christ would sup
He drained the dregs from out my cup:
So how should I be lifted up?'

'Thou shalt win Glory.'
'In the skies,
Lord Jesus, cover up mine eyes
Lest they should look on vanities.'

'Thou shalt have Knowledge.'
'Helpless dust!
In Thee, O Lord, I put my trust:
Answer Thou for me, Wise and Just.'

'And Might.'—
'Get thee behind me. Lord,
Who hast redeemed and not abhorred
My soul, oh keep it by Thy Word.'

THE ONE CERTAINTY

SONNET

VANITY of vanities, the Preacher saith,
All things are vanity. The eye and ear
Cannot be filled with what they see and hear.
Like early dew, or like the sudden breath
Of wind, or like the grass that withereth,
Is man, tossed to and fro by hope and fear :
So little joy hath he, so little cheer,
Till all things end in the long dust of death.
To-day is still the same as yesterday,
To-morrow also even as one of them ;
And there is nothing new under the sun :
Until the ancient race of Time be run,
The old thorns shall grow out of the old stem
And morning shall be cold and twilight grey.

CHRISTIAN AND JEW

A DIALOGUE

'OH happy happy land !
Angels like rushes stand
About the wells of light.'—
'Alas, I have not eyes for this fair sight :
Hold fast my hand.'—

‘ As in a soft wind, they
Bend all one blessed way,
Each bowed in his own glory, star with star.’—
‘ I cannot see so far,
Here shadows are.’—

‘ White-winged the cherubim,
Yet whiter seraphim,
Glow white with intense fire of love.’—
‘ Mine eyes are dim :
I look in vain above,
And miss their hymn.’—

‘ Angels, Archangels cry
One to other ceaselessly
(I hear them sing)
One “ Holy, Holy, Holy ” to their King.’—
‘ I do not hear them, I.’—

‘ At one side Paradise
Is curtained from the rest,
Made green for wearied eyes ;
Much softer than the breast
Of mother-dove clad in a rainbow’s dyes.

‘ All precious souls are there
Most safe, elect by grace,
All tears are wiped for ever from their face :
Untired in prayer
They wait and praise
Hidden for a little space.

'Boughs of the Living Vine
They spread in summer shine
  Green leaf with leaf:
Sap of the Royal Vine it stirs like wine
  In all both less and chief.

'Sing to the Lord,
  All spirits of all flesh, sing;
For He hath not abhorred
  Our low estate nor scorn'd our offering:
  Shout to our King.'—

'But Zion said:
  My Lord forgetteth me.
Lo, she hath made her bed
  In dust; forsaken weepeth she
  Where alien rivers swell the sea.

'She laid her body as the ground,
  Her tender body as the ground to those
Who passed; her harpstrings cannot sound
In a strange land; discrowned
  She sits, and drunk with woes.'—

'O drunken not with wine,
  Whose sins and sorrows have fulfilled the sum,—
  Be not afraid, arise, be no more dumb;
Arise, shine,
  For thy light is come.'—

'Can these bones live?'—
'God knows:
The prophet saw such clothed with flesh and skin;
A wind blew on them and life entered in;
They shook and rose.
Hasten the time, O Lord, blot out their sin,
Let life begin.'

SWEET DEATH

The sweetest blossoms die.
And so it was that, going day by day
Unto the Church to praise and pray,
And crossing the green churchyard thoughtfully,
I saw how on the graves the flowers
Shed their fresh leaves in showers,
And how their perfume rose up to the sky
Before it passed away.

The youngest blossoms die.
They die and fall and nourish the rich earth
From which they lately had their birth;
Sweet life, but sweeter death that passeth by
And is as though it had not been:—
All colours turn to green;
The bright hues vanish and the odours fly,
The grass hath lasting worth.

And youth and beauty die.
  So be it, O my God, Thou God of truth:
  Better than beauty and than youth
Are Saints and Angels, a glad company;
  And Thou, O Lord, our Rest and Ease,
  Art better far than these.
Why should we shrink from our full harvest? why
  Prefer to glean with Ruth?

SYMBOLS

I WATCHED a rosebud very long
  Brought on by dew and sun and shower,
  Waiting to see the perfect flower:
Then, when I thought it should be strong,
  It opened at the matin hour
And fell at evensong.

I watched a nest from day to day,
  A green nest full of pleasant shade,
  Wherein three speckled eggs were laid:
But when they should have hatched in May,
  The two old birds had grown afraid
Or tired, and flew away.

Then in my wrath I broke the bough
  That I had tended so with care,
  Hoping its scent should fill the air;

I crushed the eggs, not heeding how
  Their ancient promise had been fair :
I would have vengeance now.

But the dead branch spoke from the sod,
  And the eggs answered me again :
  Because we failed dost thou complain ?
Is thy wrath just ? And what if God,
  Who waiteth for thy fruits in vain,
Should also take the rod ?

'CONSIDER THE LILIES OF THE FIELD'

FLOWERS preach to us if we will hear :—
The rose saith in the dewy morn :
I am most fair ;
Yet all my loveliness is born
Upon a thorn.
The poppy saith amid the corn :
Let but my scarlet head appear
And I am held in scorn ;
Yet juice of subtle virtue lies
Within my cup of curious dyes.
The lilies say : Behold how we
Preach without words of purity.
The violets whisper from the shade
Which their own leaves have made :
Men scent our fragrance on the air,
Yet take no heed
Of humble lessons we would read.

But not alone the fairest flowers :
The merest grass
Along the roadside where we pass,
Lichen and moss and sturdy weed,
Tell of His love who sends the dew,
The rain and sunshine too,
To nourish one small seed.

THE WORLD

SONNET

By day she woos me, soft, exceeding fair :
But all night as the moon so changeth she ;
Loathsome and foul with hideous leprosy
And subtle serpents gliding in her hair.
By day she woos me to the outer air,
Ripe fruits, sweet flowers, and full satiety :
But through the night, a beast she grins at me,
A very monster void of love and prayer.
By day she stands a lie : by night she stands
In all the naked horror of the truth
With pushing horns and clawed and clutching hands.
Is this a friend indeed ; that I should sell
My soul to her, give her my life and youth,
Till my feet, cloven too, take hold on hell ?

A TESTIMONY

I SAID of laughter: it is vain.
Of mirth I said: what profits it?
Therefore I found a book, and writ
Therein how ease and also pain,
How health and sickness, every one
Is vanity beneath the sun.

Man walks in a vain shadow; he
Disquieteth himself in vain.
The things that were shall be again;
The rivers do not fill the sea,
But turn back to their secret source;
The winds too turn upon their course.

Our treasures moth and rust corrupt,
Or thieves break through and steal, or they
Make themselves wings and fly away.
One man made merry as he supped,
Nor guessed how when that night grew dim
His soul would be required of him.

We build our houses on the sand
Comely withoutside and within;
But when the winds and rains begin
To beat on them, they cannot stand:
They perish, quickly overthrown,
Loose from the very basement stone.

All things are vanity, I said:
  Yea vanity of vanities.
  The rich man dies; and the poor dies:
The worms feeds sweetly on the dead.
Whate'er thou lackest, keep this trust:
All in the end shall have but dust:

The one inheritance, which best
  And worst alike shall find and share:
  The wicked cease from troubling there,
And there the weary be at rest;
There all the wisdom of the wise
Is vanity of vanities.

Man flourishes as a green leaf
  And as a leaf doth pass away;
  Or as a shade that cannot stay
And leaves no track, his course is brief:
Yet man doth hope and fear and plan
Till he is dead:—oh foolish man!

Our eyes cannot be satisfied
  With seeing, nor our ears be filled
  With hearing: yet we plant and build
And buy and make our borders wide;
We gather wealth, we gather care,
But know not who shall be our heir.

Why should we hasten to arise
  So early, and so late take rest?
  Our labour is not good; our best

Hopes fade ; our heart is stayed on lies :
Verily, we sow wind ; and we
Shall reap the whirlwind, verily.

He who hath little shall not lack ;
  He who hath plenty shall decay .
  Our fathers went ; we pass away ;
Our children follow on our track :
So generations fail, and so
They are renewed and come and go.

The earth is fattened with our dead ;
  She swallows more and doth not cease :
  Therefore her wine and oil increase
And her sheaves are not numberèd ;
Therefore her plants are green, and all
Her pleasant trees lusty and tall.

Therefore the maidens cease to sing,
  And the young men are very sad ;
  Therefore the sowing is not glad,
And mournful is the harvesting.
Of high and low, of great and small,
Vanity is the lot of all.

A King dwelt in Jerusalem ;
  He was the wisest man on earth ;
  He had all riches from his birth,
And pleasures till he tired of them ;
Then, having tested all things, he
Witnessed that all are vanity.

SLEEP AT SEA

SOUND the deep waters :—
  Who shall sound that deep ?—
Too short the plummet,
  And the watchmen sleep.
Some dream of effort
  Up a toilsome steep ;
Some dream of pasture grounds
  For harmless sheep.

White shapes flit to and fro
  From mast to mast ;
They feel the distant tempest
  That nears them fast :
Great rocks are straight ahead,
  Great shoals not past ;
They shout to one another
  Upon the blast.

Oh, soft the streams drop music
  Between the hills,
And musical the birds' nests
  Beside those rills :
The nests are types of home
  Love-hidden from ills,
The nests are types of spirits
  Love-music fills.

So dream the sleepers,
  Each man in his place ;
The lightning shows the smile
  Upon each face :
The ship is driving, driving,
  It drives apace :
And sleepers smile, and spirits
  Bewail their case.

The lightning glares and reddens
  Across the skies ;
It seems but sunset
  To those sleeping eyes.
When did the sun go down
  On such a wise ?
From such a sunset
  When shall day arise ?

'Wake,' call the spirits :
  But to heedless ears :
They have forgotten sorrows
  And hopes and fears ;
They have forgotten perils
  And smiles and tears ;
Their dream has held them long,
  Long years and years.

'Wake,' call the spirits again :
  But it would take
A louder summons
  To bid them awake.

Some dream of pleasure
  For another's sake ;
Some dream, forgetful
  Of a lifelong ache.

One by one slowly,
  Ah, how sad and slow !
Wailing and praying
  The spirits rise and go :
Clear stainless spirits
  White as white as snow ;
Pale spirits, wailing
  For an overthrow.

One by one flitting,
  Like a mournful bird
Whose song is tired at last
  For no mate heard.
The loving voice is silent,
  The useless word ;
One by one flitting
  Sick with hope deferred.

Driving and driving,
  The ship drives amain :
While swift from mast to mast
  Shapes flit again,
Flit silent as the silence
  Where men lie slain ;
Their shadow cast upon the sails
  Is like a stain.

No voice to call the sleepers,
  No hand to raise :
They sleep to death in dreaming,
  Of length of days.
Vanity of vanities,
  The Preacher says :
Vanity is the end
  Of all their ways.

FROM HOUSE TO HOME

The first was like a dream through summer heat,
  The second like a tedious numbing swoon,
While the half-frozen pulses lagged to beat
  Beneath a winter moon.

'But,' says my friend, 'what was this thing and where ?'
  It was a pleasure-place within my soul ;
An earthly paradise supremely fair
  That lured me from the goal.

The first part was a tissue of hugged lies ;
  The second was its ruin fraught with pain :
Why raise the fair delusion to the skies
  But to be dashed again ?

My castle stood of white transparent glass
  Glittering and frail with many a fretted spire,
But when the summer sunset came to pass
  It kindled into fire.

My pleasaunce was an undulating green,
  Stately with trees whose shadows slept below,
With glimpses of smooth garden-beds between
  Like flame or sky or snow.

Swift squirrels on the pastures took their ease,
  With leaping lambs safe from the unfeared knife ;
All singing-birds rejoicing in those trees
  Fulfilled their careless life.

Woodpigeons cooed there, stockdoves nestled there;
  My trees were full of songs and flowers and fruit,
Their branches spread a city to the air
  And mice lodged in their root.

My heath lay farther off, where lizards lived
  In strange metallic mail, just spied and gone ;
Like darted lightnings here and there perceived
  But nowhere dwelt upon.

Frogs and fat toads were there to hop or plod
  And propagate in peace, an uncouth crew,
Where velvet-headed rushes rustling nod
  And spill the morning dew.

All caterpillars throve beneath my rule,
  With snails and slugs in corners out of sight ;
I never marred the curious sudden stool
  That perfects in a night.

Safe in his excavated gallery
  The burrowing mole groped on from year to year;
No harmless hedgehog curled because of me
  His prickly back for fear.

Oft times one like an angel walked with me,
  With spirit-discerning eyes like flames of fire,
But deep as the unfathomed endless sea
  Fulfilling my desire :

And sometimes like a snowdrift he was fair,
  And sometimes like a sunset glorious red,
And sometimes he had wings to scale the air
  With aureole round his head.

We sang our songs together by the way,
  Calls and recalls and echoes of delight ;
So communed we together all the day,
  And so in dreams by night.

I have no words to tell what way we walked,
  What unforgotten path now closed and sealed ;
I have no words to tell all things we talked,
  All things that he revealed :

This only can I tell : that hour by hour
  I waxed more feastful, lifted up and glad ;
I felt no thorn-prick when I plucked a flower,
  Felt not my friend was sad.

'To-morrow,' once I said to him with smiles:
'To-night,' he answered gravely and was dumb,
But pointed out the stones that numbered miles
And miles and miles to come.

'Not so,' I said: 'to-morrow shall be sweet;
To-night is not so sweet as coming days.'
Then first I saw that he had turned his feet,
Had turned from me his face:

Running and flying miles and miles he went,
But once looked back to beckon with his hand
And cry: 'Come home, O love, from banishment:
Come to the distant land.'

That night destroyed me like an avalanche;
One night turned all my summer back to snow:
Next morning not a bird upon my branch,
Not a lamb woke below,—

No bird, no lamb, no living breathing thing;
No squirrel scampered on my breezy lawn,
No mouse lodged by his hoard: all joys took wing
And fled before that dawn.

Azure and sun were starved from heaven above,
No dew had fallen, but biting frost lay hoar:
O love, I knew that I should meet my love,
Should find my love no more.

'My love no more,' I muttered stunned with pain :
  I shed no tear, I wrung no passionate hand,
Till something whispered : 'You shall meet again,
  Meet in a distant land.'

Then with a cry like famine I arose,
  I lit my candle, searched from room to room,
Searched up and down ; a war of winds that froze
  Swept through the blank of gloom.

I searched day after day, night after night ;
  Scant change there came to me of night or day :
'No more,' I wailed, 'no more :' and trimmed my light,
  And gnashed but did not pray,

Until my heart broke and my spirit broke :
  Upon the frost-bound floor I stumbled, fell,
And moaned : 'It is enough : withhold the stroke,
  Farewell, O love, farewell.'

Then life swooned from me. And I heard the song
  Of spheres and spirits rejoicing over me :
One cried : 'Our sister, she hath suffered long.'—
  One answered : 'Make her see.'—

One cried : 'Oh blessèd she who no more pain,
  Who no more disappointment shall receive.'—
One answered : 'Not so : she must live again ;
  Strengthen thou her to live.'

So while I lay entranced a curtain seemed
  To shrivel with crackling from before my face ;
Across mine eyes a waxing radiance beamed
  And showed a certain place.

I saw a vision of a woman, where
  Night and new morning strive for domination ;
Incomparably pale, and almost fair,
  And sad beyond expression.

Her eyes were like some fire-enshrining gem,
  Were stately like the stars, and yet were tender ;
Her figure charmed me like a windy stem
  Quivering and drooped and slender.

I stood upon the outer barren ground,
  She stood on inner ground that budded flowers ;
While circling in their never-slackening round
  Danced by the mystic hours.

But every flower was lifted on a thorn,
  And every thorn shot upright from its sands
To gall her feet ; hoarse laughter pealed in scorn
  With cruel clapping hands.

She bled and wept, yet did not shrink ; her strength
  Was strung up until daybreak of delight :
She measured measureless sorrow toward its length,
  And breadth, and depth, and height.

Then marked I how a chain sustained her form,
A chain of living links not made nor riven :
It stretched sheer up through lightning, wind, and storm,
And anchored fast in heaven.

One cried : 'How long ? yet founded on the Rock
She shall do battle, suffer, and attain.'—
One answered : 'Faith quakes in the tempest shock :
Strengthen her soul again.'

I saw a cup sent down and come to her
Brimfull of loathing and of bitterness :
She drank with livid lips that seemed to stir
The depth, not make it less.

But as she drank I spied a hand distil
New wine and virgin honey ; making it
First bitter-sweet, then sweet indeed, until
She tasted only sweet.

Her lips and cheeks waxed rosy-fresh and young ;
Drinking she sang: 'My soul shall nothing want;'
And drank anew : while soft a song was sung,
A mystical slow chant.

One cried : 'The wounds are faithful of a friend :
The wilderness shall blossom as a rose.'—
One answered : 'Rend the veil, declare the end,
Strengthen her ere she goes.'

Then earth and heaven were rolled up like a scroll ;
  Time and space, change and death, had passed away ;
Weight, number, measure, each had reached its whole ;
  The day had come, that day.

Multitudes—multitudes—stood up in bliss,
  Made equal to the angels, glorious, fair ;
With harps, palms, wedding-garments, kiss of peace,
  And crowned and haloed hair.

They sang a song, a new song in the height,
  Harping with harps to Him Who is Strong and True :
They drank new wine, their eyes saw with new light,
  Lo, all things were made new.

Tier beyond tier they rose and rose and rose
  So high that it was dreadful, flames with flames :
No man could number them, no tongue disclose
  Their secret sacred names.

As though one pulse stirred all, one rush of blood
  Fed all, one breath swept through them myriad-voiced,
They struck their harps, cast down their crowns, they stood
  And worshipped and rejoiced.

Each face looked one way like a moon new-lit,
Each face looked one way towards its Sun of Love;
Drank love and bathed in love and mirrored it
And knew no end thereof.

Glory touched glory on each blessèd head,
Hands locked dear hands never to sunder more:
These were the new-begotten from the dead
Whom the great birthday bore.

Heart answered heart, soul answered soul at rest,
Double against each other, filled, sufficed:
All loving, loved of all; but loving best
And best beloved of Christ.

I saw that one who lost her love in pain,
Who trod on thorns, who drank the loathsome cup;
The lost in night, in day was found again;
The fallen was lifted up.

They stood together in the blessèd noon,
They sang together through the length of days;
Each loving face bent Sunwards like a moon
New-lit with love and praise.

Therefore, O friend, I would not if I might
Rebuild my house of lies, wherein I joyed
One time to dwell: my soul shall walk in white,
Cast down but not destroyed.

Therefore in patience I possess my soul;
  Yea, therefore as a flint I set my face,
To pluck down, to build up again the whole—
  But in a distant place.

These thorns are sharp, yet I can tread on them;
  This cup is loathsome, yet He makes it sweet:
My face is steadfast toward Jerusalem,
  My heart remembers it.

I lift the hanging hands, the feeble knees—
  I, precious more than seven times molten gold—
Until the day when from His storehouses
  God shall bring new and old;

Beauty for ashes, oil of joy for grief,
  Garment of praise for spirit of heaviness:
Although to-day I fade as doth a leaf,
  I languish and grow less.

Although to-day He prunes my twigs with pain,
  Yet doth His blood nourish and warm my root:
To-morrow I shall put forth buds again
  And clothe myself with fruit.

Although to-day I walk in tedious ways,
  To-day His staff is turned into a rod,
Yet will I wait for Him the appointed days
  And stay upon my God.

OLD AND NEW YEAR DITTIES

1

NEW Year met me somewhat sad:
  Old Year leaves me tired,
Stripped of favourite things I had,
  Baulked of much desired:
Yet farther on my road to-day
God willing, farther on my way.

New Year coming on apace
  What have you to give me?
Bring you scathe, or bring you grace,
Face me with an honest face;
  You shall not deceive me:
Be it good or ill, be it what you will,
It needs shall help me on my road,
My rugged way to heaven, please God.

2

WATCH with me, men, women, and children dear,
You whom I love, for whom I hope and fear,
Watch with me this last vigil of the year.
Some hug their business, some their pleasure-scheme;
Some seize the vacant hour to sleep or dream;
Heart locked in heart some kneel and watch apart.

Watch with me blessèd spirits, who delight
All through the holy night to walk in white,
Or take your ease after the long-drawn fight.
I know not if they watch with me : I know
They count this eve of resurrection slow,
And cry, 'How long ?' with urgent utterance strong.

Watch with me Jesus, in my loneliness :
Though others say me nay, yet say Thou yes ;
Though others pass me by, stop Thou to bless.
Yea, Thou dost stop with me this vigil night ;
To-night of pain, to-morrow of delight :
I, Love, am Thine ; Thou, Lord my God, art mine.

3

Passing away, saith the World, passing away :
Chances, beauty and youth sapped day by day :
Thy life never continueth in one stay.
Is the eye waxen dim, is the dark hair changing to grey
That hath won neither laurel nor bay ?
I shall clothe myself in Spring and bud in May :
Thou, root-stricken, shalt not rebuild thy decay
On my bosom for aye.
Then I answered : Yea.

Passing away, saith my Soul, passing away :
With its burden of fear and hope, of labour and play ;

Hearken what the past doth witness and say:
Rust in thy gold, a moth is in thine array,
A canker is in thy bud, thy leaf must decay.
At midnight, at cockcrow, at morning, one certain day
Lo, the Bridegroom shall come and shall not delay:
Watch thou and pray.
Then I answered: Yea.

Passing away, saith my God, passing away:
Winter passeth after the long delay:
New grapes on the vine, new figs on the tender spray,
Turtle calleth turtle in Heaven's May.
Though I tarry wait for Me, trust Me, watch and pray.
Arise, come away, night is past and lo it is day,
My love, My sister, My spouse, thou shalt hear Me say.
Then I answered: Yea.

AMEN

It is over. What is over?
  Nay, how much is over truly!—
Harvest days we toiled to sow for;
  Now the sheaves are gathered newly,
  Now the wheat is garnered duly.

It is finished. What is finished?
  Much is finished known or unknown:
Lives are finished; time diminished;
  Was the fallow field left unsown?
  Will these buds be always unblown?

It suffices. What suffices?
  All suffices reckoned rightly:
Spring shall bloom where now the ice is,
  Roses make the bramble sightly,
  And the quickening sun shine brightly,
  And the latter wind blow lightly,
And my garden teem with spices.

THE PRINCE'S PROGRESS, AND OTHER POEMS, 1866

THE PRINCE'S PROGRESS

TILL all sweet gums and juices flow,
Till the blossom of blossoms blow,
The long hours go and come and go,
  The bride she sleepeth, waketh, sleepeth,
Waiting for one whose coming is slow :—
    Hark ! the bride weepeth.

'How long shall I wait, come heat come rime ?'—
'Till the strong Prince comes, who must come in time'
(Her women say), 'there's a mountain to climb,
  A river to ford. Sleep, dream and sleep ;
Sleep' (they say) : 'we've muffled the chime,
    Better dream than weep.'

In his world-end palace the strong Prince sat,
Taking his ease on cushion and mat,
Close at hand lay his staff and his hat.
  'When wilt thou start ? the bride waits, O youth.'—
'Now the moon's at full ; I tarried for that,
    Now I start in truth.

'But tell me first, true voice of my doom,
Of my veiled bride in her maiden bloom;
Keeps she watch through glare and through gloom,
  Watch for me asleep and awake?'—
'Spell-bound she watches in one white room,
    And is patient for thy sake.

'By her head lilies and rosebuds grow;
The lilies droop, will the rosebuds blow?
The silver slim lilies hang the head low;
  Their stream is scanty, their sunshine rare:
Let the sun blaze out, and let the stream flow,
    They will blossom and wax fair.

'Red and white poppies grow at her feet,
The blood-red wait for sweet summer heat,
Wrapped in bud-coats hairy and neat;
  But the white buds swell, one day they will burst,
Will open their death-cups drowsy and sweet—
    Which will open the first?'

Then a hundred sad voices lifted a wail,
And a hundred glad voices piped on the gale:
'Time is short, life is short,' they took up the tale:
  'Life is sweet, love is sweet, use to-day while you
      may;
Love is sweet, and to-morrow may fail;
    Love is sweet, use to-day.'

While the song swept by, beseeching and meek,
Up rose the Prince with a flush on his cheek,
Up he rose to stir and to seek,

Going forth in the joy of his strength;
Strong of limb if of purpose weak,
Starting at length.

Forth he set in the breezy morn,
Crossing green fields of nodding corn,
As goodly a Prince as ever was born;
Carolling with the carolling lark;—
Sure his bride will be won and worn,
Ere fall of the dark.

So light his step, so merry his smile,
A milkmaid loitered beside a stile,
Set down her pail and rested awhile,
A wave-haired milkmaid, rosy and white;
The Prince, who had journeyed at least a mile,
Grew athirst at the sight.

'Will you give me a morning draught?'—
'You're kindly welcome,' she said, and laughed.
He lifted the pail, new milk he quaffed;
Then wiping his curly black beard like silk:
'Whitest cow that ever was calved
Surely gave you this milk.'

Was it milk now, or was it cream?
Was she a maid, or an evil dream?
Her eyes began to glitter and gleam;
He would have gone, but he stayed instead;
Green they gleamed as he looked in them:
'Give me my fee,' she said.—

'I will give you a jewel of gold.'—
'Not so; gold is heavy and cold.'—
'I will give you a velvet fold
  Of foreign work your beauty to deck.'—
'Better I like my kerchief rolled
    Light and white round my neck.'—

'Nay,' cried he, 'but fix your own fee.'—
She laughed, 'You may give the full moon to me;
Or else sit under this apple-tree
  Here for one idle day by my side;
After that I'll let you go free,
    And the world is wide.'

Loth to stay, but to leave her slack,
He half turned away, then he quite turned back:
For courtesy's sake he could not lack
  To redeem his own royal pledge;
Ahead too the windy heaven lowered black
    With a fire-cloven edge.

So he stretched his length in the apple-tree shade,
Lay and laughed and talked to the maid,
Who twisted her hair in a cunning braid
  And writhed it shining in serpent-coils,
And held him a day and night fast laid
    In her subtle toils.

At the death of night and the birth of day,
When the owl left off his sober play,
And the bat hung himself out of the way,

Woke the song of mavis and merle,
And heaven put off its hodden grey
For mother-o'-pearl.

Peeped up daisies here and there,
Here, there, and everywhere;
Rose a hopeful lark in the air,
Spreading out towards the sun his breast;
While the moon set solemn and fair
Away in the West.

'Up, up, up,' called the watchman lark,
In his clear réveillée: 'Hearken, oh hark!
Press to the high goal, fly to the mark.
Up, O sluggard, new morn is born;
If still asleep when the night falls dark,
Thou must wait a second morn.'

'Up, up, up,' sad glad voices swelled:
'So the tree falls and lies as it's felled.
Be thy bands loosed, O sleeper, long held
In sweet sleep whose end is not sweet.
Be the slackness girt and the softness quelled
And the slowness fleet.'

Off he set. The grass grew rare,
A blight lurked in the darkening air,
The very moss grew hueless and spare,
The last daisy stood all astunt;
Behind his back the soil lay bare,
But barer in front.

A land of chasm and rent, a land
Of rugged blackness on either hand:
If water trickled its track was tanned
  With an edge of rust to the chink;
If one stamped on stone or on sand
    It returned a clink.

A lifeless land, a loveless land,
Without lair or nest on either hand:
Only scorpions jerked in the sand,
  Black as black iron, or dusty pale;
From point to point sheer rock was manned
    By scorpions in mail.

A land of neither life nor death,
Where no man buildeth or fashioneth,
Where none draws living or dying breath;
  No man cometh or goeth there,
No man doeth, seeketh, saith,
    In the stagnant air.

Some old volcanic upset must
Have rent the crust and blackened the crust;
Wrenched and ribbed it beneath its dust
  Above earth's molten centre at seethe,
Heaved and heaped it by huge upthrust
    Of fire beneath.

Untrodden before, untrodden since:
Tedious land for a social Prince;
Halting, he scanned the outs and ins,

Endless, labyrinthine, grim,
Of the solitude that made him wince,
Laying wait for him.

By bulging rock and gaping cleft,
Even of half mere daylight reft,
Rueful he peered to right and left,
Muttering in his altered mood :
'The fate is hard that weaves my weft,
Though my lot be good.'

Dim the changes of day to night,
Of night scarce dark to day not bright.
Still his road wound towards the right,
Still he went, and still he went,
Till one night he espied a light,
In his discontent.

Out it flashed from a yawn-mouthed cave,
Like a red-hot eye from a grave.
No man stood there of whom to crave
Rest for wayfarer plodding by :
Though the tenant were churl or knave
The Prince might try.

In he passed and tarried not,
Groping his way from spot to spot,
Towards where the cavern flare glowed hot :—
An old, old mortal, cramped and double,
Was peering into a seething-pot,
In a world of trouble.

The veriest atomy he looked,
With grimy fingers clutching and crooked,
Tight skin, a nose all bony and hooked,
And a shaking, sharp, suspicious way;
His blinking eyes had scarcely brooked
The light of day.

Stared the Prince, for the sight was new;
Stared, but asked without more ado:
'May a weary traveller lodge with you,
Old father, here in your lair?
In your country the inns seem few,
And scanty the fare.'

The head turned not to hear him speak;
The old voice whistled as through a leak
(Out it came in a quavering squeak):
'Work for wage is a bargain fit:
If there's aught of mine that you seek
You must work for it.

'Buried alive from light and air
This year is the hundredth year,
I feed my fire with a sleepless care,
Watching my potion wane or wax:
Elixir of Life is simmering there,
And but one thing lacks.

'If you're fain to lodge here with me,
Take that pair of bellows you see—
Too heavy for my old hands they be—

Take the bellows and puff and puff:
When the steam curls rosy and free
The broth's boiled enough.

'Then take your choice of all I have;
I will give you life if you crave.
Already I'm mildewed for the grave,
So first myself I must drink my fill:
But all the rest may be yours, to save
Whomever you will.'

'Done,' quoth the Prince, and the bargain stood.
First he piled on resinous wood,
Next plied the bellows in hopeful mood;
Thinking, 'My love and I will live.
If I tarry, why life is good,
And she may forgive.'

The pot began to bubble and boil;
The old man cast in essence and oil,
He stirred all up with a triple coil
Of gold and silver and iron wire,
Dredged in a pinch of virgin soil,
And fed the fire.

But still the steam curled watery white;
Night turned to day and day to night;
One thing lacked, by his feeble sight
Unseen, unguessed by his feeble mind:
Life might miss him, but Death the blight
Was sure to find.

So when the hundredth year was full
The thread was cut and finished the school.
Death snapped the old worn-out tool,
  Snapped him short while he stood and stirred
(Though stiff he stood as a stiff-necked mule)
    With never a word.

Thus at length the old crab was nipped.
The dead hand slipped, the dead finger dipped
In the broth as the dead man slipped,—
  That same instant, a rosy red
Flushed the steam, and quivered and clipped
    Round the dead old head.

The last ingredient was supplied
(Unless the dead man mistook or lied).
Up started the Prince, he cast aside
  The bellows plied through the tedious trial,
Made sure that his host had died,
    And filled a phial.

'One night's rest,' thought the Prince: 'This done,
Forth I start with the rising sun:
With the morrow I rise and run,
  Come what will of wind or of weather.
This draught of Life when my Bride is won
    We'll drink together.'

Thus the dead man stayed in his grave,
Self-chosen, the dead man in his cave;
There he stayed, were he fool or knave,

  Or honest seeker who had not found :
While the Prince outside was prompt to crave
    Sleep on the ground.

' If she watches, go bid her sleep ;
Bid her sleep, for the road is steep :
He can sleep who holdeth her cheap,
  Sleep and wake and sleep again.
Let him sow, one day he shall reap,
    Let him sow the grain.

' When there blows a sweet garden rose,
Let it bloom and wither if no man knows :
But if one knows when the sweet thing blows,
  Knows, and lets it open and drop,
If but a nettle his garden grows
    He hath earned the crop.'

Through his sleep the summons rang,
Into his ears it sobbed and it sang.
Slow he woke with a drowsy pang,
  Shook himself without much debate,
Turned where he saw green branches hang,
    Started though late.

For the black land was travelled o'er,
He should see the grim land no more.
A flowering country stretched before
  His face when the lovely day came back :
He hugged the phial of Life he bore,
    And resumed his track.

By willow courses he took his path,
Spied what a nest the kingfisher hath,
Marked the fields green to aftermath,
  Marked where the red-brown field-mouse ran,
Loitered a while for a deep-stream bath,
    Yawned for a fellow-man.

Up on the hills not a soul in view,
In the vale not many nor few;
Leaves, still leaves, and nothing new.
  It's oh for a second maiden, at least,
To bear the flagon, and taste it too,
    And flavour the feast.

Lagging he moved, and apt to swerve;
Lazy of limb, but quick of nerve.
At length the water-bed took a curve,
  The deep river swept its bankside bare;
Waters streamed from the hill-reserve—
    Waters here, waters there.

High above, and deep below,
Bursting, bubbling, swelling the flow,
Like hill torrents after the snow,—
  Bubbling, gurgling, in whirling strife,
Swaying, sweeping, to and fro,—
    He must swim for his life.

Which way?—which way?—his eyes grew dim
With the dizzying whirl—which way to swim?
The thunderous downshoot deafened him;

Half he choked in the lashing spray:
Life is sweet, and the grave is grim—
Which way?—which way?

A flash of light, a shout from the strand:
'This way—this way; here lies the land!'
His phial clutched in one drowning hand;
He catches—misses—catches a rope;
His feet slip on the slipping sand:
Is there life?—is there hope?

Just saved, without pulse or breath,—
Scarcely saved from the gulp of death;
Laid where a willow shadoweth—
Laid where a swelling turf is smooth.
(O Bride! but the Bridegroom lingereth
For all thy sweet youth.)

Kind hands do and undo,
Kind voices whisper and coo:
'I will chafe his hands'—'And I'—'And you
Raise his head, put his hair aside.'
(If many laugh, one well may rue:
Sleep on, thou Bride.)

So the Prince was tended with care:
One wrung foul ooze from his clustered hair·
Two chafed his hands, and did not spare;
But one held his drooping head breast-high,
Till his eyes oped, and at unaware
They met eye to eye.

Oh, a moon face in a shadowy place,
And a light touch and a winsome grace,
And a thrilling tender voice that says:
 'Safe from waters that seek the sea—
Cold waters by rugged ways—
  Safe with me.'

While overhead bird whistles to bird,
And round about plays a gamesome herd:
'Safe with us'—some take up the word—
 'Safe with us, dear lord and friend:
All the sweeter if long deferred
  Is rest in the end.'

Had he stayed to weigh and to scan,
He had been more or less than a man:
He did what a young man can,
 Spoke of toil and an arduous way—
Toil to-morrow, while golden ran
  The sands of to-day.

Slip past, slip fast,
Uncounted hours from first to last,
Many hours till the last is past,
 Many hours dwindling to one—
One hour whose die is cast,
  One last hour gone.

Come, gone—gone for ever—
Gone as an unreturning river—
Gone as to death the merriest liver—

Gone as the year at the dying fall—
To-morrow, to-day, yesterday, never—
Gone once for all.

Came at length the starting-day,
With last words, and last last words to say,
With bodiless cries from far away—
Chiding wailing voices that rang
Like a trumpet-call to the tug and fray;
And thus they sang:

'Is there life?—the lamp burns low;
Is there hope?—the coming is slow:
The promise promised so long ago,
The long promise, has not been kept.
Does she live?—does she die?—she slumbers so
Who so oft has wept.

'Does she live?—does she die?—she languisheth
As a lily drooping to death,
As a drought-worn bird with failing breath,
As a lovely vine without a stay,
As a tree whereof the owner saith,
"Hew it down to-day."'

Stung by that word the Prince was fain
To start on his tedious road again.
He crossed the stream where a ford was plain,
He clomb the opposite bank though steep,
And swore to himself to strain and attain
Ere he tasted sleep.

Huge before him a mountain frowned
With foot of rock on the valley ground,
And head with snows incessant crowned,
  And a cloud mantle about its strength,
And a path which the wild goat hath not found
    In its breadth and length.

But he was strong to do and dare:
If a host had withstood him there,
He had braved a host with little care
  In his lusty youth and his pride,
Tough to grapple though weak to snare.
    He comes, O Bride.

Up he went where the goat scarce clings,
Up where the eagle folds her wings,
Past the green line of living things,
  Where the sun cannot warm the cold,—
Up he went as a flame enrings
    Where there seems no hold.

Up a fissure barren and black,
Till the eagles tired upon his track,
And the clouds were left behind his back,
  Up till the utmost peak was past,
Then he gasped for breath and his strength fell slack;
    He paused at last.

Before his face a valley spread
Where fatness laughed, wine, oil, and bread,
Where all fruit-trees their sweetness shed,

Where all birds made love to their kind,
Where jewels twinkled, and gold lay red
And not hard to find.

Midway down the mountain side
(On its green slope the path was wide)
Stood a house for a royal bride,
Built all of changing opal stone,
The royal palace, till now descried
In his dreams alone.

Less bold than in days of yore,
Doubting now though never before,
Doubting he goes and lags the more :
Is the time late ? does the day grow dim ?
Rose, will she open the crimson core
Of her heart to him ?

Take heart of grace ! the potion of Life
May go far to woo him a wife :
If she frown, yet a lover's strife
Lightly raised can be laid again :
A hasty word is never the knife
To cut love in twain.

Far away stretched the royal land,
Fed by dew, by a spice-wind fanned :
Light labour more, and his foot would stand
On the threshold, all labour done ;
Easy pleasure laid at his hand,
And the dear Bride won.

His slackening steps pause at the gate—
Does she wake or sleep ?—the time is late—
Does she sleep now, or watch and wait ?
  She has watched, she has waited long,
Watching athwart the golden grate
    With a patient song.

Fling the golden portals wide,
The Bridegroom comes to his promised Bride ;
Draw the gold-stiff curtains aside,
  Let them look on each other's face,
She in her meekness, he in his pride—
    Day wears apace.

Day is over, the day that wore.
What is this that comes through the door,
The face covered, the feet before ?
  This that coming takes his breath ;
This Bride not seen, to be seen no more
    Save of Bridegroom Death ?

Veiled figures carrying her
Sweep by yet make no stir ;
There is a smell of spice and myrrh,
  A bride-chant burdened with one name ;
The bride-song rises steadier
    Than the torches' flame :

'Too late for love, too late for joy,
  Too late, too late !

You loitered on the road too long,
  You trifled at the gate:
The enchanted dove upon her branch
  Died without a mate;
The enchanted princess in her tower
  Slept, died, behind the grate;
Her heart was starving all this while
  You made it wait.

'Ten years ago, five years ago,
  One year ago,
Even then you had arrived in time,
  Though somewhat slow;
Then you had known her living face
  Which now you cannot know:
The frozen fountain would have leaped,
  The buds gone on to blow,
The warm south wind would have awaked
  To melt the snow.

'Is she fair now as she lies?
  Once she was fair;
Meet queen for any kingly king,
  With gold-dust on her hair.
Now these are poppies in her locks,
  White poppies she must wear;
Must wear a veil to shroud her face
  And the want graven there:
Or is the hunger fed at length,
  Cast off the care?

'We never saw her with a smile
  Or with a frown;
Her bed seemed never soft to her,
  Though tossed of down;
She little heeded what she wore,
  Kirtle, or wreath, or gown;
We think her white brows often ached
  Beneath her crown,
Till silvery hairs showed in her locks
  That used to be so brown.

'We never heard her speak in haste:
  Her tones were sweet,
And modulated just so much
  As it was meet:
Her heart sat silent through the noise
  And concourse of the street.
There was no hurry in her hands,
  No hurry in her feet;
There was no bliss drew nigh to her,
  That she might run to greet.

'You should have wept her yesterday,
  Wasting upon her bed:
But wherefore should you weep to-day
  That she is dead?
Lo, we who love weep not to-day,
  But crown her royal head.
Let be these poppies that we strew,
  Your roses are too red:
Let be these poppies, not for you
  Cut down and spread.'

MAIDEN-SONG

LONG ago and long ago,
  And long ago still,
There dwelt three merry maidens
  Upon a distant hill.
One was tall Meggan,
  And one was dainty May,
But one was fair Margaret,
  More fair than I can say,
Long ago and long ago.

When Meggan plucked the thorny rose,
  And when May pulled the brier,
Half the birds would swoop to see,
  Half the beasts draw nigher ;
Half the fishes of the streams
  Would dart up to admire :
But when Margaret plucked a flag-flower,
  Or poppy hot aflame,
All the beasts and all the birds
  And all the fishes came
To her hand more soft than snow.

Strawberry leaves and May-dew
  In brisk morning air,
Strawberry leaves and May-dew
  Make maidens fair.

'I go for strawberry leaves,'
  Meggan said one day:
'Fair Margaret can bide at home,
  But you come with me, May;
Up the hill and down the hill,
  Along the winding way
You and I are used to go.'

So these two fair sisters
  Went with innocent will
Up the hill and down again,
  And round the homestead hill:
While the fairest sat at home,
  Margaret like a queen,
Like a blush-rose, like the moon
  In her heavenly sheen,
Fragrant-breathed as milky cow
  Or field of blossoming bean,
Graceful as an ivy bough
  Born to cling and lean;
Thus she sat to sing and sew.

When she raised her lustrous eyes
  A beast peeped at the door;
When she downward cast her eyes
  A fish gasped on the floor;
When she turned away her eyes
  A bird perched on the sill,
Warbling out its heart of love,
  Warbling warbling still,
With pathetic pleadings low.

Light-foot May with Meggan
  Sought the choicest spot,
Clothed with thyme-alternate grass:
  Then, while day waxed hot,
Sat at ease to play and rest,
  A gracious rest and play;
The loveliest maidens near or far,
  When Margaret was away,
Who sat at home to sing and sew.

Sun-glow flushed their comely cheeks,
  Wind-play tossed their hair,
Creeping things among the grass
  Stroked them here and there;
Meggan piped a merry note,
  A fitful wayward lay,
While shrill as bird on topmost twig
  Piped merry May;
Honey-smooth the double flow.

Sped a herdsman from the vale,
  Mounting like a flame,
All on fire to hear and see,
  With floating locks he came.
Looked neither north nor south,
  Neither east nor west,
But sat him down at Meggan's feet
  As love-bird on his nest,
And wooed her with a silent awe,
  With trouble not expressed;

She sang the tears into his eyes,
  The heart out of his breast:
So he loved her, listening so.

She sang the heart out of his breast,
  The words out of his tongue;
Hand and foot and pulse he paused
  Till her song was sung.
Then he spoke up from his place
  Simple words and true:
'Scanty goods have I to give,
  Scanty skill to woo;
But I have a will to work,
  And a heart for you:
Bid me stay or bid me go.'

Then Meggan mused within herself:
  'Better be first with him,
Than dwell where fairer Margaret sits,
  Who shines my brightness dim,
For ever second where she sits,
  However fair I be:
I will be lady of his love,
  And he shall worship me;
I will be lady of his herds
  And stoop to his degree,
At home where kids and fatlings grow.'

Sped a shepherd from the height
  Headlong down to look,
(White lambs followed, lured by love
  Of their shepherd's crook):

He turned neither east nor west,
  Neither north nor south,
But knelt right down to May, for love
  Of her sweet-singing mouth ;
Forgot his flocks, his panting flocks
  In parching hill-side drouth ;
Forgot himself for weal or woe.

Trilled her song and swelled her song
  With maiden coy caprice
In a labyrinth of throbs,
  Pauses, cadences ;
Clear-noted as a dropping brook,
  Soft-noted like the bees,
Wild-noted as the shivering wind
  Forlorn through forest trees :
Love-noted like the wood-pigeon
  Who hides herself for love,
Yet cannot keep her secret safe,
  But coos and coos thereof :
Thus the notes rang loud or low.

He hung breathless on her breath ;
  Speechless, who listened well ;
Could not speak or think or wish
  Till silence broke the spell.
Then he spoke, and spread his hands,
  Pointing here and there :
'See my sheep and see the lambs,
  Twin lambs which they bare.

All myself I offer you,
  All my flocks and care,
Your sweet song hath moved me so.'

In her fluttered heart young May
  Mused a dubious while :
'If he loves me as he says'—
  Her lips curved with a smile :
'Where Margaret shines like the sun
  I shine but like a moon ;
If sister Meggan makes her choice
  I can make mine as soon ;
At cockcrow we were sister-maids,
  We may be brides at noon.'
Said Meggan, 'Yes ;' May said not 'No.'

Fair Margaret stayed alone at home,
  Awhile she sang her song,
Awhile sat silent, then she thought :
  'My sisters loiter long.'
That sultry noon had waned away,
  Shadows had waxen great :
'Surely,' she thought within herself,
  'My sisters loiter late.'
She rose, and peered out at the door,
  With patient heart to wait,
And heard a distant nightingale
  Complaining of its mate ;
Then down the garden slope she walked,
  Down to the garden gate,
Leaned on the rail and waited so.

The slope was lightened by her eyes
  Like summer lightning fair,
Like rising of the haloed moon
  Lightened her glimmering hair,
While her face lightened like the sun
  Whose dawn is rosy white.
Thus crowned with maiden majesty
  She peered into the night,
Looked up the hill and down the hill,
  To left hand and to right,
Flashing like fire-flies to and fro.

Waiting thus in weariness
  She marked the nightingale
Telling, if any one would heed,
  Its old complaining tale.
Then lifted she her voice and sang,
  Answering the bird :
Then lifted she her voice and sang,
  Such notes were never heard
From any bird when Spring's in blow.

The king of all that country
  Coursing far, coursing near,
Curbed his amber-bitted steed,
  Coursed amain to hear ;
All his princes in his train,
  Squire, and knight, and peer,
With his crown upon his head,
  His sceptre in his hand,

Down he fell at Margaret's knees
  Lord king of all that land,
To her highness bending low.

Every beast and bird and fish
  Came mustering to the sound,
Every man and every maid
  From miles of country round:
Meggan on her herdsman's arm,
  With her shepherd May,
Flocks and herds trooped at their heels
  Along the hill-side way;
No foot too feeble for the ascent,
  Not any head too grey;
Some were swift and none were slow.

So Margaret sang her sisters home
  In their marriage mirth;
Sang free birds out of the sky,
  Beasts along the earth,
Sang up fishes of the deep—
  All breathing things that move
Sang from far and sang from near
  To her lovely love;
Sang together friend and foe;

Sang a golden-bearded king
  Straightway to her feet,
Sang him silent where he knelt
  In eager anguish sweet.
But when the clear voice died away,
  When longest echoes died,

He stood up like a royal man
  And claimed her for his bride.
So three maids were wooed and won
  In a brief May-tide,
Long ago and long ago.

JESSIE CAMERON

'Jessie, Jessie Cameron,
  Hear me but this once,' quoth he.
'Good luck go with you, neighbour's son,
  But I'm no mate for you,' quoth she.
Day was verging toward the night
  There beside the moaning sea,
Dimness overtook the light
  There where the breakers be.
'O Jessie, Jessie Cameron,
  I have loved you long and true.'—
'Good luck go with you, neighbour's son,
  But I'm no mate for you.'

She was a careless, fearless girl,
  And made her answer plain,
Outspoken she to earl or churl,
  Kindhearted in the main,
But somewhat heedless with her tongue
  And apt at causing pain;
A mirthful maiden she and young,
  Most fair for bliss or bane.

'Oh, long ago I told you so,
  I tell you so to-day:
Go you your way, and let me go
  Just my own free way.'

The sea swept in with moan and foam
  Quickening the stretch of sand;
They stood almost in sight of home;
  He strove to take her hand.
'Oh, can't you take your answer then,
  And won't you understand?
For me you're not the man of men,
  I've other plans are planned.
You're good for Madge, or good for Cis,
  Or good for Kate, may be:
But what's to me the good of this
  While you're not good for me?'

They stood together on the beach,
  They two alone,
And louder waxed his urgent speech,
  His patience almost gone:
'Oh, say but one kind word to me,
  Jessie, Jessie Cameron.'—
'I'd be too proud to beg,' quoth she,
  And pride was in her tone.
And pride was in her lifted head,
  And in her angry eye,
And in her foot, which might have fled
  But would not fly.

Some say that he had gipsy blood,
  That in his heart was guile:
Yet he had gone through fire and flood
  Only to win her smile.
Some say his grandam was a witch,
  A black witch from beyond the Nile,
Who kept an image in a niche
  And talked with it the while.
And by her hut far down the lane
  Some say they would not pass at night,
Lest they should hear an unked strain
  Or see an unked sight.

Alas, for Jessie Cameron!—
  The sea crept moaning, moaning nigher:
She should have hastened to begone,—
  The sea swept higher, breaking by her:
She should have hastened to her home
  While yet the west was flushed with fire,
But now her feet are in the foam,
  The sea-foam sweeping higher.
O mother, linger at your door,
  And light your lamp to make it plain,
But Jessie she comes home no more,
  No more again.

They stood together on the strand,
  They only each by each;
Home, her home, was close at hand,
  Utterly out of reach.

Her mother in the chimney nook
  Heard a startled sea-gull screech,
But never turned her head to look
  Towards the darkening beach :
Neighbours here and neighbours there
  Heard one scream, as if a bird
Shrilly screaming cleft the air :—
  That was all they heard.

Jessie she comes home no more,
  Comes home never ;
Her lover's step sounds at his door
  No more for ever.
And boats may search upon the sea
  And search along the river,
But none know where the bodies be :
  Sea-winds that shiver,
Sea-birds that breast the blast,
  Sea-waves swelling,
Keep the secret first and last
  Of their dwelling.

Whether the tide so hemmed them round
  With its pitiless flow,
That when they would have gone they found
  No way to go ;
Whether she scorned him to the last
  With words flung to and fro,
Or clung to him when hope was past,
  None will ever know :

Whether he helped or hindered her,
Threw up his life or lost it well,
The troubled sea for all its stir
Finds no voice to tell.

Only watchers by the dying
Have thought they heard one pray
Wordless, urgent ; and replying
One seem to say him nay :
And watchers by the dead have heard
A windy swell from miles away,
With sobs and screams, but not a word
Distinct for them to say :
And watchers out at sea have caught
Glimpse of a pale gleam here or there,
Come and gone as quick as thought,
Which might be hand or hair.

SPRING QUIET

GONE were but the Winter,
Come were but the Spring,
I would go to a covert
Where the birds sing;

Where in the whitethorn
Singeth a thrush,
And a robin sings
In the holly-bush.

Full of fresh scents
  Are the budding boughs
Arching high over
  A cool green house :

Full of sweet scents,
  And whispering air
Which sayeth softly :
  ' We spread no snare ;

' Here dwell in safety,
  Here dwell alone,
With a clear stream
  And a mossy stone.

' Here the sun shineth
  Most shadily ;
Here is heard an echo
  Of the far sea,
  Though far off it be.'

THE POOR GHOST

' OH whence do you come, my dear friend, to me,
With your golden hair all fallen below your knee,
And your face as white as snowdrops on the lea,
And your voice as hollow as the hollow sea ? '

' From the other world I come back to you,
My locks are uncurled with dripping drenching dew.
You know the old, whilst I know the new :
But to-morrow you shall know this too.'

'Oh not to-morrow into the dark, I pray;
Oh not to-morrow, too soon to go away:
Here I feel warm and well-content and gay:
Give me another year, another day.'

'Am I so changed in a day and a night
That mine own only love shrinks from me with fright,
Is fain to turn away to left or right
And cover up his eyes from the sight?'

'Indeed I loved you, my chosen friend,
I loved you for life, but life has an end;
Through sickness I was ready to tend:
But death mars all, which we cannot mend.

'Indeed I loved you; I love you yet,
If you will stay where your bed is set,
Where I have planted a violet,
Which the wind waves, which the dew makes wet.'

'Life is gone, then love too is gone,
It was a reed that I leant upon:
Never doubt I will leave you alone
And not wake you rattling bone with bone.

'I go home alone to my bed,
Dug deep at the foot and deep at the head,
Roofed in with a load of lead,
Warm enough for the forgotten dead.

'But why did your tears soak through the clay,
And why did your sobs wake me where I lay?
I was away, far enough away:
Let me sleep now till the Judgment Day.'

A PORTRAIT

I

She gave up beauty in her tender youth,
Gave all her hope and joy and pleasant ways ;
She covered up her eyes lest they should gaze
On vanity, and chose the bitter truth.
Harsh towards herself, towards others full of ruth,
Servant of servants, little known to praise,
Long prayers and fasts trenched on her nights and days :
She schooled herself to sights and sounds uncouth
That with the poor and stricken she might make
A home, until the least of all sufficed
Her wants ; her own self learned she to forsake,
Counting all earthly gain but hurt and loss.
So with calm will she chose and bore the cross
And hated all for love of Jesus Christ.

II

They knelt in silent anguish by her bed,
And could not weep ; but calmly there she lay.
All pain had left her ; and the sun's last ray
Shone through upon her, warming into red
The shady curtains. In her heart she said :
'Heaven opens ; I leave these and go away ;
The Bridegroom calls,—shall the Bride seek to stay ?'
Then low upon her breast she bowed her head.

O lily flower, O gem of priceless worth,
O dove with patient voice and patient eyes,
O fruitful vine amid a land of dearth,
O maid replete with loving purities,
Thou bowedst down thy head with friends on earth
To raise it with the saints in Paradise.

DREAM-LOVE

Young Love lies sleeping
In May-time of the year,
Among the lilies,
Lapped in the tender light:
White lambs come grazing,
White doves come building there;
And round about him
The May-bushes are white.

Soft moss the pillow
For oh, a softer cheek;
Broad leaves cast shadow
Upon the heavy eyes:
There winds and waters
Grow lulled and scarcely speak;
There twilight lingers
The longest in the skies.

Young Love lies dreaming;
But who shall tell the dream?
A perfect sunlight
On rustling forest tips;

Or perfect moonlight
  Upon a rippling stream ;
Or perfect silence,
  Or song of cherished lips.

Burn odours round him
  To fill the drowsy air ;
Weave silent dances
  Around him to and fro ;
For oh, in waking
  The sights are not so fair,
And song and silence
  Are not like these below.

Young Love lies dreaming
  Till summer days are gone,—
Dreaming and drowsing
  Away to perfect sleep :
He sees the beauty
  Sun hath not looked upon,
And tastes the fountain
  Unutterably deep.

Him perfect music
  Doth hush unto his rest,
And through the pauses
  The perfect silence calms :
Oh, poor the voices
  Of earth from east to west,
And poor earth's stillness
  Between her stately palms.

Young Love lies drowsing
  Away to poppied death;
Cool shadows deepen
  Across the sleeping face:
So fails the summer
  With warm, delicious breath;
And what hath autumn
  To give us in its place?

Draw close the curtains
  Of branched evergreen;
Change cannot touch them
  With fading fingers sere:
Here the first violets
  Perhaps will bud unseen,
And a dove, may be,
  Return to nestle here.

TWICE

I TOOK my heart in my hand
  (O my love, O my love),
I said: Let me fall or stand,
  Let me live or die,
But this once hear me speak—
  (O my love, O my love)—
Yet a woman's words are weak;
  You should speak, not I.

You took my heart in your hand
  With a friendly smile,
With a critical eye you scanned,
  Then set it down,
And said: It is still unripe,
  Better wait awhile;
Wait while the skylarks pipe,
  Till the corn grows brown.

As you set it down it broke—
  Broke, but I did not wince;
I smiled at the speech you spoke,
  At your judgment that I heard:
But I have not often smiled
  Since then, nor questioned since,
Nor cared for corn-flowers wild,
  Nor sung with the singing bird.

I take my heart in my hand,
  O my God, O my God,
My broken heart in my hand:
  Thou hast seen, judge Thou.
My hope was written on sand,
  O my God, O my God:
Now let Thy judgment stand—
  Yea, judge me now.

This contemned of a man,
  This marred one heedless day,
This heart take Thou to scan
  Both within and without:

Refine with fire its gold,
  Purge Thou its dross away—
Yea, hold it in Thy hold,
  Whence none can pluck it out.

I take my heart in my hand—
  I shall not die, but live—
Before Thy face I stand;
  I, for Thou callest such:
All that I have I bring,
  All that I am I give,
Smile Thou and I shall sing,
  But shall not question much.

SONGS IN A CORNFIELD

A SONG in a cornfield
  Where corn begins to fall,
Where reapers are reaping,
  Reaping one, reaping all.
Sing pretty Lettice,
  Sing Rachel, sing May;
Only Marian cannot sing
  While her sweetheart's away.

Where is he gone to
  And why does he stay?
He came across the green sea
  But for a day,
Across the deep green sea
  To help with the hay.

His hair was curly yellow
  And his eyes were grey,
He laughed a merry laugh
  And said a sweet say.
Where is he gone to
  That he comes not home?
To-day or to-morrow
  He surely will come.
Let him haste to joy
  Lest he lag for sorrow,
For one weeps to-day
  Who'll not weep to-morrow:
To-day she must weep
  For gnawing sorrow,
To-night she may sleep
  And not wake to-morrow.

May sang with Rachel
  In the waxing warm weather,
Lettice sang with them,
  They sang all together:—

'Take the wheat in your arm
  Whilst day is broad above,
Take the wheat to your bosom,
  But not a false false love.
  Out in the fields
    Summer heat gloweth,
  Out in the fields
    Summer wind bloweth,

Out in the fields
Summer friend showeth,
Out in the fields
Summer wheat groweth;
But in the winter
When summer heat is dead
And summer wind has veered
And summer friend has fled,
Only summer wheat remaineth,
White cakes and bread.
Take the wheat, clasp the wheat
That's food for maid and dove;
Take the wheat to your bosom,
But not a false false love.'

A silence of full noontide heat
Grew on them at their toil:
The farmer's dog woke up from sleep,
The green snake hid her coil.
Where grass stood thickest, bird and beast
Sought shadows as they could,
The reaping men and women paused
And sat down where they stood;
They ate and drank and were refreshed,
For rest from toil is good.

While the reapers took their ease,
Their sickles lying by,
Rachel sang a second strain,
And singing seemed to sigh:—

'There goes the swallow—
Could we but follow!
  Hasty swallow stay,
  Point us out the way;
Look back swallow, turn back swallow, stop swallow.

'There went the swallow—
Too late to follow:
  Lost our note of way,
  Lost our chance to-day;
Good bye swallow, sunny swallow, wise swallow.

'After the swallow
All sweet things follow:
  All things go their way,
  Only we must stay,
Must not follow; good bye swallow, good swallow.'

Then listless Marian raised her head
  Among the nodding sheaves;
Her voice was sweeter than that voice;
  She sang like one who grieves:
Her voice was sweeter than its wont
  Among the nodding sheaves;
All wondered while they heard her sing
  Like one who hopes and grieves:—

'Deeper than the hail can smite,
Deeper than the frost can bite,
Deep asleep through day and night,
  Our delight.

'Now thy sleep no pang can break,
No to-morrow bid thee wake,
Not our sobs who sit and ache
For thy sake.

'Is it dark or light below?
Oh, but is it cold like snow?
Dost thou feel the green things grow
Fast or slow?

'Is it warm or cold beneath,
Oh, but is it cold like death?
Cold like death, without a breath,
Cold like death?'

If he comes to-day
He will find her weeping;
If he comes to-morrow
He will find her sleeping;
If he comes the next day
He'll not find her at all,
He may tear his curling hair,
Beat his breast and call.

A YEAR'S WINDFALLS

On the wind of January
  Down flits the snow,
Travelling from the frozen North
  As cold as it can blow.
Poor robin redbreast,
  Look where he comes ;
Let him in to feel your fire,
  And toss him of your crumbs.

On the wind in February
  Snowflakes float still,
Half inclined to turn to rain,
  Nipping, dripping, chill.
Then the thaws swell the streams,
  And swollen rivers swell the sea :—
If the winter ever ends
  How pleasant it will be.

In the wind of windy March
  The catkins drop down,
Curly, caterpillar-like,
  Curious green and brown.
With concourse of nest-building birds
  And leaf-buds by the way,
We begin to think of flowers
  And life and nuts some day.

With the gusts of April
  Rich fruit-tree blossoms fall,
On the hedged-in orchard-green,
  From the southern wall.
Apple-trees and pear-trees
  Shed petals white or pink,
Plum-trees and peach-trees ;
  While sharp showers sink and sink.

Little brings the May breeze
  Beside pure scent of flowers,
While all things wax and nothing wanes
  In lengthening daylight hours.
Across the hyacinth beds
  The wind lags warm and sweet,
Across the hawthorn tops,
  Across the blades of wheat.

In the wind of sunny June
  Thrives the red rose crop,
Every day fresh blossoms blow
  While the first leaves drop ;
White rose and yellow rose
  And moss-rose choice to find,
And the cottage cabbage-rose
  Not one whit behind.

On the blast of scorched July
  Drives the pelting hail,
From thunderous lightning-clouds, that blot
  Blue heaven grown lurid-pale.

Weedy waves are tossed ashore,
  Sea-things strange to sight
Gasp upon the barren shore
  And fade away in light.

In the parching August wind
  Corn-fields bow the head,
Sheltered in round valley depths,
  On low hills outspread.
Early leaves drop loitering down
  Weightless on the breeze,
First fruits of the year's decay
  From the withering trees.

In brisk wind of September
  The heavy-headed fruits
Shake upon their bending boughs
  And drop from the shoots ;
Some glow golden in the sun,
  Some show green and streaked,
Some set forth a purple bloom,
  Some blush rosy-cheeked.

In strong blast of October
  At the equinox,
Stirred up in his hollow bed
  Broad ocean rocks ;
Plunge the ships on his bosom,
  Leaps and plunges the foam,—
It's oh ! for mothers' sons at sea,
  That they were safe at home.

In slack wind of November
  The fog forms and shifts;
All the world comes out again
  When the fog lifts.
Loosened from their sapless twigs
  Leaves drop with every gust;
Drifting, rustling, out of sight
  In the damp or dust.

Last of all, December,
  The year's sands nearly run,
Speeds on the shortest day,
  Curtails the sun;
With its bleak raw wind
  Lays the last leaves low,
Brings back the nightly frosts,
  Brings back the snow.

THE QUEEN OF HEARTS

How comes it, Flora, that, whenever we
Play cards together, you invariably,
    However the pack parts,
    Still hold the Queen of Hearts?

I've scanned you with a scrutinizing gaze,
Resolved to fathom these your secret ways:
    But, sift them as I will,
    Your ways are secret still.

I cut and shuffle ; shuffle, cut, again ;
But all my cutting, shuffling, proves in vain :
Vain hope, vain forethought too ;
That Queen still falls to you.

I dropped her once, prepense ; but, ere the deal
Was dealt, your instinct seemed her loss to feel :
'There should be one card more,'
You said, and searched the floor.

I cheated once ; I made a private notch
In Heart-Queen's back, and kept a lynx-eyed watch ;
Yet such another back
Deceived me in the pack :

The Queen of Clubs assumed by arts unknown
An imitative dint that seemed my own ;
This notch, not of my doing,
Misled me to my ruin.

It baffles me to puzzle out the clue,
Which must be skill, or craft, or luck in you :
Unless, indeed, it be
Natural affinity.

ONE DAY

I WILL tell you when they met:
In the limpid days of Spring;
Elder boughs were budding yet,
Oaken boughs looked wintry still,
But primrose and veined violet
In the mossful turf were set,
While meeting birds made haste to sing
And build with right good will.

I will tell you when they parted:
When plenteous Autumn sheaves were brown,
Then they parted heavy-hearted;
The full rejoicing sun looked down
As grand as in the days before;
Only they had lost a crown;
Only to them those days of yore
Could come back nevermore.

When shall they meet? I cannot tell,
Indeed, when they shall meet again,
Except some day in Paradise:
For this they wait, one waits in pain.
Beyond the sea of death love lies
For ever, yesterday, to-day;
Angels shall ask them, 'Is it well?'
And they shall answer, 'Yea.'

A BIRD'S-EYE VIEW

'Croak, croak, croak,'
Thus the Raven spoke,
Perched on his crooked tree
As hoarse as hoarse could be.
Shun him and fear him,
Lest the Bridegroom hear him;
Scout him and rout him
With his ominous eye about him.

Yet, 'Croak, croak, croak,'
Still tolled from the oak;
From that fatal black bird,
Whether heard or unheard:
'O ship upon the high seas,
Freighted with lives and spices,
Sink, O ship,' croaked the Raven:
'Let the Bride mount to heaven.'

In a far foreign land
Upon the wave-edged sand,
Some friends gaze wistfully
Across the glittering sea.
'If we could clasp our sister,'
Three say, 'now we have missed her!'
'If we could kiss our daughter!'
Two sigh across the water.

Oh, the ship sails fast
With silken flags at the mast,
And the home-wind blows soft;
But a Raven sits aloft,
Chuckling and choking,
Croaking, croaking, croaking:—
Let the beacon-fire blaze higher;
Bridegroom, watch; the Bride draws nigher.

On a sloped sandy beach,
Which the spring-tide billows reach,
Stand a watchful throng
Who have hoped and waited long:
'Fie on this ship, that tarries
With the priceless freight it carries.
The time seems long and longer:
O languid wind, wax stronger;'—

Whilst the Raven perched at ease
Still croaks and does not cease,
One monotonous note
Tolled from his iron throat:
'No father, no mother,
But I have a sable brother:
He sees where ocean flows to,
And he knows what he knows too.'

A day and a night
They kept watch worn and white;
A night and a day
For the swift ship on its way:

For the Bride and her maidens
—Clear chimes the bridal cadence—
For the tall ship that never
Hove in sight for ever.

On either shore, some
Stand in grief loud or dumb
As the dreadful dread
Grows certain though unsaid.
For laughter there is weeping,
And waking instead of sleeping,
And a desperate sorrow
Morrow after morrow.

Oh, who knows the truth,
How she perished in her youth,
And like a queen went down
Pale in her royal crown :
How she went up to glory
From the sea-foam chill and hoary,
From the sea-depth black and riven
To the calm that is in Heaven ?

They went down, all the crew,
The silks and spices too,
The great ones and the small,
One and all, one and all.
Was it through stress of weather,
Quicksands, rocks, or all together ?
Only the Raven knows this,
And he will not disclose this.—

After a day and year
The bridal bells chime clear;
After a year and a day
The Bridegroom is brave and gay:
Love is sound, faith is rotten;
The old Bride is forgotten:—
Two ominous Ravens only
Remember, black and lonely.

LIGHT LOVE

'Oh, sad thy lot before I came,
  But sadder when I go;
My presence but a flash of flame,
  A transitory glow
  Between two barren wastes like snow.
What wilt thou do when I am gone,
  Where wilt thou rest, my dear?
For cold thy bed to rest upon,
  And cold the falling year
  Whose withered leaves are lost and sere.'

She hushed the baby at her breast,
  She rocked it on her knee:
'And I will rest my lonely rest,
  Warmed with the thought of thee,
  Rest lulled to rest by memory.'
She hushed the baby with her kiss,
  She hushed it with her breast;

'Is death so sadder much than this—
  Sure death that builds a nest
  For those who elsewhere cannot rest?'

'Oh, sad thy note, my mateless dove,
  With tender nestling cold;
But hast thou ne'er another love
  Left from the days of old,
  To build thy nest of silk and gold,
To warm thy paleness to a blush
  When I am far away—
To warm thy coldness to a flush,
  And turn thee back to May,
  And turn thy twilight back to day?'

She did not answer him again,
  But leaned her face aside,
Weary with the pang of shame and pain,
  And sore with wounded pride:
  He knew his very soul had lied.
She strained his baby in her arms,
  His baby to her heart:
'Even let it go, the love that harms:
  We twain will never part;
  Mine own, his own, how dear thou art.'

'Now never teaze me, tender-eyed,
  Sigh-voiced,' he said in scorn:
'For nigh at hand there blooms a bride,
  My bride before the morn;
  Ripe-blooming she, as thou forlorn.

Ripe-blooming she, my rose, my peach;
  She wooes me day and night:
I watch her tremble in my reach;
  She reddens, my delight,
  She ripens, reddens in my sight.'

'And is she like a sunlit rose?
  Am I like withered leaves?
Haste where thy spicèd garden blows:
  But in bare Autumn eves
  Wilt thou have store of harvest sheaves?
Thou leavest love, true love behind,
  To seek a love as true;
Go, seek in haste: but wilt thou find?
  Change new again for new;
  Pluck up, enjoy—yea, trample too.

'Alas for her, poor faded rose,
  Alas for her, like me,
Cast down and trampled in the snows.'
  'Like thee? nay, not like thee:
  She leans, but from a guarded tree.
Farewell, and dream as long ago,
  Before we ever met:
Farewell; my swift-paced horse seems slow.'
  She raised her eyes, not wet
  But hard, to Heaven: 'Does God forget?'

A DREAM

SONNET

ONCE in a dream (for once I dreamed of you)
We stood together in an open field ;
Above our heads two swift-winged pigeons wheeled,
Sporting at ease and courting full in view.
When loftier still a broadening darkness flew,
Down-swooping, and a ravenous hawk revealed ;
Too weak to fight, too fond to fly, they yield ;
So farewell life and love and pleasures new.
Then as their plumes fell fluttering to the ground,
Their snow-white plumage flecked with crimson drops,
I wept, and thought I turned towards you to weep :
But you were gone ; while rustling hedgerow tops
Bent in a wind which bore to me a sound
Of far-off piteous bleat of lambs and sheep.

A RING POSY

JESS and Jill are pretty girls,
Plump and well to do,
In a cloud of windy curls :
Yet I know who
Loves me more than curls or pearls

I'm not pretty, not a bit—
  Thin and sallow-pale ;
When I trudge along the street
  I don't need a veil :
Yet I have one fancy hit.

Jess and Jill can trill and sing
  With a flute-like voice,
Dance as light as bird on wing,
  Laugh for careless joys :
Yet it's I who wear the ring.

Jess and Jill will mate some day,
  Surely, surely :
Ripen on to June through May,
While the sun shines make their hay,
  Slacken steps demurely :
Yet even there I lead the way.

BEAUTY IS VAIN

WHILE roses are so red,
  While lilies are so white,
Shall a woman exalt her face
  Because it gives delight ?
She 's not so sweet as a rose,
  A lily 's straighter than she,
And if she were as red or white
  She 'd be but one of three.

Whether she flush in love's summer
Or in its winter grow pale,
Whether she flaunt her beauty
Or hide it away in a veil,
Be she red or white,
And stand she erect or bowed,
Time will win the race he runs with her
And hide her away in a shroud.

LADY MAGGIE

You must not call me Maggie, you must not call me Dear,
For I'm Lady of the Manor now stately to see;
And if there comes a babe, as there may some happy year,
'Twill be little lord or lady at my knee.

Oh, but what ails you, my sailor cousin Phil,
That you shake and turn white like a cockcrow ghost?
You're as white as I turned once down by the mill,
When one told me you and ship and crew were lost:

Philip my playfellow, when we were boy and girl
(It was the Miller's Nancy told it to me),
Philip with the merry life in lip and curl,
Philip my playfellow drowned in the sea!

I thought I should have fainted, but I did not faint;
I stood stunned at the moment, scarcely sad,
Till I raised my wail of desolate complaint
For you, my cousin, brother, all I had.

They said I looked so pale—some say so fair—
My lord stopped in passing to soothe me back to life:
I know I missed a ringlet from my hair
Next morning; and now I am his wife.

Look at my gown, Philip, and look at my ring,
I'm all crimson and gold from top to toe:
All day long I sit in the sun and sing,
Where in the sun red roses blush and blow.

And I'm the rose of roses says my lord;
And to him I'm more than the sun in the sky,
While I hold him fast with the golden cord
Of a curl, with the eyelash of an eye.

His mother said 'fie,' and his sisters cried 'shame,'
His highborn ladies cried 'shame' from their place:
They said 'fie' when they only heard my name,
But fell silent when they saw my face.

Am I so fair, Philip? Philip, did you think
I was so fair when we played boy and girl,
Where blue forget-me-nots bloomed on the brink
Of our stream which the mill-wheel sent awhirl?

If I was fair then sure I'm fairer now,
  Sitting where a score of servants stand,
With a coronet on high days for my brow
  And almost a sceptre for my hand.

You're but a sailor, Philip, weatherbeaten brown,
  A stranger on land and at home on the sea,
Coasting as best you may from town to town:
  Coasting along do you often think of me?

I'm a great lady in a sheltered bower,
  With hands grown white through having nought to do:
Yet sometimes I think of you hour after hour
  Till I nigh wish myself a child with you.

WHAT WOULD I GIVE?

What would I give for a heart of flesh to warm me through,
Instead of this heart of stone ice-cold whatever I do;
Hard and cold and small, of all hearts the worst of all.

What would I give for words, if only words would come;
But now in its misery my spirit has fallen dumb:
Oh, merry friends, go your way, I have never a word to say.

What would I give for tears, not smiles but scalding tears,
To wash the black mark clean, and to thaw the frost of years,
To wash the stain ingrain and to make me clean again.

THE BOURNE

UNDERNEATH the growing grass,
Underneath the living flowers,
Deeper than the sound of showers :
There we shall not count the hours
By the shadows as they pass.

Youth and health will be but vain,
Beauty reckoned of no worth :
There a very little girth
Can hold round what once the earth
Seemed too narrow to contain.

SUMMER

WINTER is cold-hearted,
Spring is yea and nay,
Autumn is a weathercock
Blown every way :
Summer days for me
When every leaf is on its tree ;

When Robin's not a beggar,
  And Jenny Wren's a bride,
And larks hang singing, singing, singing,
  Over the wheat-fields wide,
  And anchored lilies ride,
And the pendulum spider
  Swings from side to side,

And blue-black beetles transact business,
  And gnats fly in a host,
And furry caterpillars hasten
  That no time be lost,
And moths grow fat and thrive,
And ladybirds arrive.

Before green apples blush,
  Before green nuts embrown,
Why, one day in the country
  Is worth a month in town ;
  Is worth a day and a year
Of the dusty, musty, lag-last fashion
  That days drone elsewhere.

AUTUMN

I DWELL alone—I dwell alone, alone,
  Whilst full my river flows down to the sea,
Gilded with flashing boats
  That bring no friend to me :
O love-songs, gurgling from a hundred throats,
  O love-pangs, let me be.

Fair fall the freighted boats which gold and stone
And spices bear to sea:
Slim, gleaming maidens swell their mellow notes,
Love-promising, entreating—
Ah! sweet, but fleeting—
Beneath the shivering, snow-white sails.
Hush! the wind flags and fails—
Hush! they will lie becalmed in sight of strand—
Sight of my strand, where I do dwell alone;
Their songs wake singing echoes in my land—
They cannot hear me moan.

One latest, solitary swallow flies
Across the sea, rough autumn-tempest tost,
Poor bird, shall it be lost?
Dropped down into this uncongenial sea,
With no kind eyes
To watch it while it dies,
Unguessed, uncared for, free:
Set free at last,
The short pang past,
In sleep, in death, in dreamless sleep locked fast.

Mine avenue is all a growth of oaks,
Some rent by thunder strokes,
Some rustling leaves and acorns in the breeze;
Fair fall my fertile trees,
That rear their goodly heads, and live at ease.

A spider's web blocks all mine avenue;
He catches down and foolish painted flies
That spider wary and wise.

Each morn it hangs a rainbow strung with dew
Betwixt boughs green with sap,
So fair, few creatures guess it is a trap:
I will not mar the web,
Though sad I am to see the small lives ebb.

It shakes—my trees shake—for a wind is roused
In cavern where it housed:
Each white and quivering sail
Of boats among the water leaves
Hollows and strains in the full-throated gale:
Each maiden sings again—
Each languid maiden, whom the calm
Had lulled to sleep with rest and spice and balm.
Miles down my river to the sea
They float and wane,
Long miles away from me.

Perhaps they say: 'She grieves,
Uplifted, like a beacon, on her tower.'
Perhaps they say: 'One hour
More, and we dance among the golden sheaves.'
Perhaps they say: 'One hour
More, and we stand,
Face to face, hand in hand;
Make haste, O slack gale, to the looked-for land!'

My trees are not in flower,
I have no bower,
And gusty creaks my tower,
And lonesome, very lonesome, is my strand.

THE GHOST'S PETITION

'THERE 's a footstep coming: look out and see,'
'The leaves are falling, the wind is calling;
No one cometh across the lea.'—

'There 's a footstep coming: O sister, look.'—
'The ripple flashes, the white foam dashes;
No one cometh across the brook.'—

'But he promised that he would come:
To-night, to-morrow, in joy or sorrow,
He must keep his word, and must come home.

'For he promised that he would come:
His word was given; from earth or heaven,
He must keep his word, and must come home.

'Go to sleep, my sweet sister Jane;
You can slumber, who need not number
Hour after hour, in doubt and pain.

'I shall sit here awhile, and watch;
Listening, hoping, for one hand groping
In deep shadow to find the latch.'

After the dark, and before the light,
One lay sleeping; and one sat weeping,
Who had watched and wept the weary night.

After the night, and before the day,
  One lay sleeping; and one sat weeping—
Watching, weeping for one away.

There came a footstep climbing the stair;
  Some one standing out on the landing
Shook the door like a puff of air—

Shook the door, and in he passed.
  Did he enter? In the room centre
Stood her husband: the door shut fast.

'O Robin, but you are cold—
  Chilled with the night-dew: so lily-white you
Look like a stray lamb from our fold.

'O Robin, but you are late:
  Come and sit near me—sit here and cheer me.'—
(Blue the flame burnt in the grate.)

'Lay not down your head on my breast:
  I cannot hold you, kind wife, nor fold you
In the shelter that you love best.

'Feel not after my clasping hand:
  I am but a shadow, come from the meadow
Where many lie, but no tree can stand.

'We are trees which have shed their leaves:
  Our heads lie low there, but no tears flow there;
Only I grieve for my wife who grieves.

'I could rest if you would not moan
  Hour after hour; I have no power
To shut my ears where I lie alone.

'I could rest if you would not cry;
  But there 's no sleeping while you sit weeping—
Watching, weeping so bitterly.'—

'Woe 's me! woe 's me! for this I have heard.
  Oh, night of sorrow!—oh, black to-morrow!
Is it thus that you keep your word?

'O you who used so to shelter me
  Warm from the least wind—why, now the east wind
Is warmer than you, whom I quake to see.

'O my husband of flesh and blood,
  For whom my mother I left, and brother,
And all I had, accounting it good,

'What do you do there, underground,
  In the dark hollow? I'm fain to follow.
What do you do there?—what have you found?'—

'What I do there I must not tell:
  But I have plenty: kind wife, content ye:
It is well with us—it is well.

'Tender hand hath made our nest;
  Our fear is ended, our hope is blended
With present pleasure, and we have rest.'—

'Oh, but Robin, I'm fain to come
  If your present days are so pleasant,
For my days are so wearisome.

'Yet I'll dry my tears for your sake:
  Why should I tease you, who cannot please you
Any more with the pains I take?'

MEMORY

I

I NURSED it in my bosom while it lived,
  I hid it in my heart when it was dead;
In joy I sat alone, even so I grieved
    Alone and nothing said.

I shut the door to face the naked truth,
  I stood alone—I faced the truth alone,
Stripped bare of self-regard or forms or ruth
    Till first and last were shown.

I took the perfect balances and weighed; 9
  No shaking of my hand disturbed the poise;
Weighed, found it wanting: not a word I said,
    But silent made my choice.

None know the choice I made ; I make it still.
None know the choice I made and broke my heart,
Breaking mine idol : I have braced my will
Once, chosen for once my part.

I broke it at a blow, I laid it cold,
Crushed in my deep heart where it used to live.
My heart dies inch by inch ; the time grows old,
Grows old in which I grieve.

II

I have a room whereinto no one enters
Save I myself alone :
There sits a blessed memory on a throne,
There my life centres.

While winter comes and goes—oh tedious comer !—
And while its nip-wind blows ;
While bloom the bloodless lily and warm rose
Of lavish summer.

If any should force entrance he might see there
One buried yet not dead,
Before whose face I no more bow my head
Or bend my knee there ;

But often in my worn life's autumn weather
I watch there with clear eyes,
And think how it will be in Paradise
When we're together.

A ROYAL PRINCESS

I, A PRINCESS, king-descended, decked with jewels, gilded, drest,
Would rather be a peasant with her baby at her breast,
For all I shine so like the sun, and am purple like the west.

Two and two my guards behind, two and two before,
Two and two on either hand, they guard me evermore;
Me, poor dove, that must not coo—eagle that must not soar.

All my fountains cast up perfumes, all my gardens grow
Scented woods and foreign spices, with all flowers in blow
That are costly, out of season as the seasons go.

All my walls are lost in mirrors, whereupon I trace
Self to right hand, self to left hand, self in every place, 11
Self-same solitary figure, self-same seeking face.

Then I have an ivory chair high to sit upon,
Almost like my father's chair, which is an ivory throne;
There I sit uplift and upright, there I sit alone.

Alone by day, alone by night, alone days without end;
My father and my mother give me treasures, search and spend—
O my father! O my mother! have you ne'er a friend?

As I am a lofty princess, so my father is
A lofty king, accomplished in all kingly subtilties,
Holding in his strong right hand world-kingdoms' balances.

He has quarrelled with his neighbours, he has scourged his foes;
Vassal counts and princes follow where his pennon goes,
Long-descended valiant lords whom the vulture knows,

On whose track the vulture swoops, when they ride in state
To break the strength of armies and topple down the great:
Each of these my courteous servant, none of these my mate.

My father counting up his strength sets down with equal pen
So many head of cattle, head of horses, head of men;
These for slaughter, these for breeding, with the how and when.

Some to work on roads, canals; some to man his
 ships;
Some to smart in mines beneath sharp overseers'
 whips;
Some to trap fur-beasts in lands where utmost
 winter nips.

Once it came into my heart, and whelmed me like
 a flood,
That these too are men and women, human flesh
 and blood;
Men with hearts and men with souls, though
 trodden down like mud.

Our feasting was not glad that night, our music
 was not gay:
On my mother's graceful head I marked a thread
 of grey,
My father frowning at the fare seemed every dish
 to weigh.

I sat beside them sole princess in my exalted place,
My ladies and my gentlemen stood by me on the
 dais:
A mirror showed me I look old and haggard in the
 face;

It showed me that my ladies all are fair to gaze upon,
Plump, plenteous-haired, to every one love's secret
 lore is known,
They laugh by day, they sleep by night; ah me,
 what is a throne?

The singing men and women sang that night as usual,
The dancers danced in pairs and sets, but music had a fall,
A melancholy windy fall as at a funeral.

Amid the toss of torches to my chamber back we swept;
My ladies loosed my golden chain; meantime I could have wept
To think of some in galling chains whether they waked or slept.

I took my bath of scented milk, delicately waited on,
They burned sweet things for my delight, cedar and cinnamon,
They lit my shaded silver lamp, and left me there alone.

A day went by, a week went by. One day I heard it said:
'Men are clamouring, women, children, clamouring to be fed;
Men like famished dogs are howling in the streets for bread.'

So two whispered by my door, not thinking I could hear,
Vulgar naked truth, ungarnished for a royal ear;
Fit for cooping in the background, not to stalk so near.

But I strained my utmost sense to catch this truth, and mark :
'There are families out grazing like cattle in the park.'
'A pair of peasants must be saved even if we build an ark.'

A merry jest, a merry laugh, each strolled upon his way ;
One was my page, a lad I reared and bore with day by day ;
One was my youngest maid as sweet and white as cream in May.

Other footsteps followed softly with a weightier tramp ;
Voices said : 'Picked soldiers have been summoned from the camp
To quell these base-born ruffians who make free to howl and stamp.'

'Howl and stamp ?' one answered : 'They made free to hurl a stone
At the minister's state coach, well aimed and stoutly thrown.'
'There 's work then for the soldiers, for this rank crop must be mown.'

'One I saw, a poor old fool with ashes on his head,
Whimpering because a girl had snatched his crust of bread :
Then he dropped ; when some one raised him, it turned out he was dead.'

'After us the deluge,' was retorted with a laugh:
'If bread 's the staff of life, they must walk without a staff.'
'While I've a loaf they're welcome to my blessing and the chaff.'

These passed. The king: stand up. Said my father with a smile:
'Daughter mine, your mother comes to sit with you awhile,
She 's sad to-day, and who but you her sadness can beguile?'

He too left me. Shall I touch my harp now while I wait,—
(I hear them doubling guard below before our palace gate—)
Or shall I work the last gold stitch into my veil of state;

Or shall my woman stand and read some unimpassioned scene,
There 's music of a lulling sort in words that pause between;
Or shall she merely fan me while I wait here for the queen?

Again I caught my father's voice in sharp word of command:
'Charge!' a clash of steel: 'Charge again, the rebels stand.
Smite and spare not, hand to hand; smite and spare not, hand to hand.'

There swelled a tumult at the gate, high voices waxing higher ;
A flash of red reflected light lit the cathedral spire ;
I heard a cry for faggots, then I heard a yell for fire.

' Sit and roast there with your meat, sit and bake there with your bread,
You who sat to see us starve,' one shrieking woman said :
' Sit on your throne and roast with your crown upon your head.'

Nay, this thing will I do, while my mother tarrieth,
I will take my fine spun gold, but not to sew therewith,
I will take my gold and gems, and rainbow fan and wreath ; 99

With a ransom in my lap, a king's ransom in my hand,
I will go down to this people, will stand face to face, will stand
Where they curse king, queen, and princess of this cursed land.

They shall take all to buy them bread, take all I have to give ;
I, if I perish, perish ; they to-day shall eat and live ;
I, if I perish, perish ; that 's the goal I half conceive :

Once to speak before the world, rend bare my heart and show
The lesson I have learned which is death, is life, to know. 107
I, if I perish, perish ; in the name of God I go.

SHALL I FORGET?

SHALL I forget on this side of the grave?
I promise nothing: you must wait and see
    Patient and brave.
(O my soul, watch with him and he with me.)

Shall I forget in peace of Paradise?
I promise nothing: follow, friend, and see
    Faithful and wise.
(O my soul, lead the way he walks with me.)

VANITY OF VANITIES

SONNET

AH, woe is me for pleasure that is vain,
  Ah, woe is me for glory that is past:
  Pleasure that bringeth sorrow at the last,
Glory that at the last bringeth no gain!
So saith the sinking heart; and so again
  It shall say till the mighty angel-blast
  Is blown, making the sun and moon aghast
And showering down the stars like sudden rain.
And evermore men shall go fearfully
  Bending beneath their weight of heaviness;
And ancient men shall lie down wearily,
  And strong men shall rise up in weariness;
Yea, even the young shall answer sighingly
  Saying one to another: How vain it is!

L. E. L.

'Whose heart was breaking for a little love.'

Downstairs I laugh, I sport and jest with all:
But in my solitary room above
I turn my face in silence to the wall;
My heart is breaking for a little love.
Though winter frosts are done,
And birds pair every one,
And leaves peep out, for springtide is begun.

I feel no spring, while spring is wellnigh blown,
I find no nest, while nests are in the grove:
Woe 's me for mine own heart that dwells alone,
My heart that breaketh for a little love.
While golden in the sun
Rivulets rise and run,
While lilies bud, for springtide is begun.

All love, are loved, save only I; their hearts
Beat warm with love and joy, beat full thereof:
They cannot guess, who play the pleasant parts,
My heart is breaking for a little love.
While beehives wake and whirr,
And rabbit thins his fur,
In living spring that sets the world astir.

I deck myself with silks and jewelry,
I plume myself like any mated dove:
They praise my rustling show, and never see
My heart is breaking for a little love.
While sprouts green lavender
With rosemary and myrrh,
For in quick spring the sap is all astir.

Perhaps some saints in glory guess the truth,
Perhaps some angels read it as they move,
And cry one to another full of ruth,
'Her heart is breaking for a little love.'
Though other things have birth,
And leap and sing for mirth,
When springtime wakes and clothes and feeds the earth.

Yet saith a saint: 'Take patience for thy scathe;'
Yet saith an angel: 'Wait, for thou shalt prove
True best is last, true life is born of death,
O thou, heart-broken for a little love.
Then love shall fill thy girth,
And love make fat thy dearth,
When new spring builds new heaven and clean new earth.'

LIFE AND DEATH

Life is not sweet. One day it will be sweet
To shut our eyes and die :
Nor feel the wild flowers blow, nor birds dart by
With flitting butterfly,
Nor grass grow long above our heads and feet,
Nor hear the happy lark that soars sky high,
Nor sigh that spring is fleet and summer fleet,
Nor mark the waxing wheat,
Nor know who sits in our accustomed seat.

Life is not good. One day it will be good
To die, then live again ;
To sleep meanwhile : so not to feel the wane
Of shrunk leaves dropping in the wood,
Nor hear the foamy lashing of the main,
Nor mark the blackened bean-fields, nor where stood
Rich ranks of golden grain
Only dead refuse stubble clothe the plain :
Asleep from risk, asleep from pain.

BIRD OR BEAST ?

Did any bird come flying
After Adam and Eve,
When the door was shut against them
And they sat down to grieve ?

I think not Eve's peacock
  Splendid to see,
And I think not Adam's eagle ;
  But a dove may be.

Did any beast come pushing
  Through the thorny hedge
Into the thorny thistly world
  Out from Eden's edge ?

I think not a lion
  Though his strength is such ;
But an innocent loving lamb
  May have done as much.

If the dove preached from her bough
  And the lamb from his sod,
The lamb and the dove
  Were preachers sent from God.

EVE

'While I sit at the door
Sick to gaze within
Mine eye weepeth sore
For sorrow and sin :
As a tree my sin stands
To darken all lands ;
Death is the fruit it bore.

'How have Eden bowers grown
Without Adam to bend them!
How have Eden flowers blown
Squandering their sweet breath
Without me to tend them!
The Tree of Life was ours,
Tree twelvefold-fruited,
Most lofty tree that flowers,
Most deeply rooted:
I chose the tree of death.

'Hadst thou but said me nay,
Adam, my brother,
I might have pined away;
I, but none other:
God might have let thee stay
Safe in our garden,
By putting me away
Beyond all pardon.

'I, Eve, sad mother
Of all who must live,
I, not another
Plucked bitterest fruit to give
My friend, husband, lover—
O wanton eyes run over;
Who but I should grieve?—
Cain hath slain his brother:
Of all who must die mother,
Miserable Eve!'

Thus she sat weeping,
Thus Eve our mother,
Where one lay sleeping
Slain by his brother.
Greatest and least
Each piteous beast
To hear her voice
Forgot his joys
And set aside his feast.

The mouse paused in his walk
And dropped his wheaten stalk;
Grave cattle wagged their heads
In rumination;
The eagle gave a cry
From his cloud station;
Larks on thyme beds
Forbore to mount or sing;
Bees drooped upon the wing;
The raven perched on high
Forgot his ration;
The conies in their rock,
A feeble nation,
Quaked sympathetical;
The mocking-bird left off to mock;
Huge camels knelt as if
In deprecation;
The kind hart's tears were falling;
Chattered the wistful stork;
Dove-voices with a dying fall

Cooed desolation
Answering grief by grief.

Only the serpent in the dust
Wriggling and crawling
Grinned an evil grin and thrust
His tongue out with its fork.

GROWN AND FLOWN

I LOVED my love from green of Spring
Until sere Autumn's fall;
But now that leaves are withering
How should one love at all?
One heart 's too small
For hunger, cold, love, everything.

I loved my love on sunny days
Until late Summer's wane;
But now that frost begins to glaze
How should one love again?
Nay, love and pain
Walk wide apart in diverse ways.

I loved my love—alas to see
That this should be, alas!
I thought that this could scarcely be,
Yet has it come to pass:
Sweet sweet love was,
Now bitter bitter grown to me.

A FARM WALK

THE year stood at its equinox
  And bluff the North was blowing,
A bleat of lambs came from the flocks,
  Green hardy things were growing;
I met a maid with shining locks
  Where milky kine were lowing.

She wore a kerchief on her neck,
  Her bare arm showed its dimple,
Her apron spread without a speck,
  Her air was frank and simple.

She milked into a wooden pail
  And sang a country ditty,
An innocent fond lovers' tale,
  That was not wise nor witty,
Pathetically rustical,
  Too pointless for the city.

She kept in time without a beat
  As true as church-bell ringers,
Unless she tapped time with her feet,
  Or squeezed it with her fingers;
Her clear unstudied notes were sweet
  As many a practised singer's.

I stood a minute out of sight,
  Stood silent for a minute
To eye the pail, and creamy white
  The frothing milk within it;

To eye the comely milking maid
  Herself so fresh and creamy:
'Good day to you,' at last I said;
  She turned her head to see me:
'Good day,' she said with lifted head;
  Her eyes looked soft and dreamy,

And all the while she milked and milked
  The grave cow heavy-laden:
I've seen grand ladies plumed and silked,
  But not a sweeter maiden;

But not a sweeter fresher maid
  Than this in homely cotton,
Whose pleasant face and silky braid
  I have not yet forgotten.

Seven springs have passed since then, as I
  Count with a sober sorrow;
Seven springs have come and passed me by,
  And spring sets in to-morrow.

I've half a mind to shake myself
  Free just for once from London,
To set my work upon the shelf
  And leave it done or undone;

To run down by the early train,
  Whirl down with shriek and whistle,
And feel the bluff North blow again,
  And mark the sprouting thistle
Set up on waste patch of the lane
  Its green and tender bristle,

And spy the scarce-blown violet banks,
  Crisp primrose leaves and others,
And watch the lambs leap at their pranks
  And butt their patient mothers.

Alas, one point in all my plan
  My serious thoughts demur to:
Seven years have passed for maid and man,
  Seven years have passed for her too;

Perhaps my rose is overblown,
  Not rosy or too rosy;
Perhaps in farmhouse of her own
  Some husband keeps her cosy,
Where I should show a face unknown.
  Good-bye, my wayside posy.

SOMEWHERE OR OTHER

SOMEWHERE or other there must surely be
  The face not seen, the voice not heard,
The heart that not yet—never yet—ah me!
    Made answer to my word.

Somewhere or other, may be near or far;
  Past land and sea, clean out of sight;
Beyond the wandering moon, beyond the star
    That tracks her night by night.

Somewhere or other, may be far or near;
  With just a wall, a hedge, between;
With just the last leaves of the dying year
    Fallen on a turf grown green

A CHILL

  WHAT can lambkins do
  All the keen night through?
Nestle by their woolly mother
  The careful ewe.

  What can nestlings do
  In the nightly dew?
Sleep beneath their mother's wing
  Till day breaks anew.

  If in field or tree
  There might only be
Such a warm soft sleeping-place
  Found for me!

CHILD'S TALK IN APRIL

I wish you were a pleasant wren,
  And I your small accepted mate;
How we'd look down on toilsome men!
  We'd rise and go to bed at eight
  Or it may be not quite so late.

Then you should see the nest I'd build,
  The wondrous nest for you and me;
The outside rough perhaps, but filled
  With wool and down; ah, you should see
  The cosy nest that it would be.

We'd have our change of hope and fear,
  Small quarrels, reconcilements sweet:
I'd perch by you to chirp and cheer,
  Or hop about on active feet
  And fetch you dainty bits to eat.

We'd be so happy by the day,
  So safe and happy through the night,
We both should feel, and I should say,
  It's all one season of delight,
And we'll make merry whilst we may.

Perhaps some day there'd be an egg
  When spring had blossomed from the snow:
I'd stand triumphant on one leg;
  Like chanticleer I'd almost crow
  To let our little neighbours know.

Next you should sit and I would sing
Through lengthening days of sunny spring :
  Till, if you wearied of the task,
I'd sit ; and you should spread your wing
  From bough to bough ; I'd sit and bask.

Fancy the breaking of the shell,
  The chirp, the chickens wet and bare,
The untried proud paternal swell ;
  And you with housewife-matron air
  Enacting choicer bills of fare.

Fancy the embryo coats of down,
  The gradual feathers soft and sleek ;
Till clothed and strong from tail to crown,
  With virgin warblings in their beak,
  They too go forth to soar and seek.

So would it last an April through
And early summer fresh with dew :
  Then should we part and live as twain,
Love-time would bring me back to you
  And build our happy nest again.

GONE FOR EVER

O HAPPY rose-bud blooming
  Upon thy parent tree,
Nay, thou art too presuming ;
For soon the earth entombing
  Thy faded charms shall be,
And the chill damp consuming.

O happy skylark springing
  Up to the broad blue sky,
Too fearless in thy winging,
Too gladsome in thy singing,
  Thou also soon shalt lie
Where no sweet notes are ringing.

And through life's shine and shower
  We shall have joy and pain ;
But in the summer bower,
And at the morning hour,
  We still shall look in vain
For the same bird and flower.

UNDER THE ROSE

'The iniquity of the fathers upon the children.'

Oh the rose of keenest thorn !
One hidden summer morn
Under the rose I was born.

I do not guess his name
Who wrought my Mother's shame,
And gave me life forlorn,
But my Mother, Mother, Mother,
I know her from all other.
My Mother pale and mild,
Fair as ever was seen,
She was but scarce sixteen,
Little more than a child.

When I was born
To work her scorn.
With secret bitter throes,
In a passion of secret woes,
She bore me under the rose.

One who my Mother nursed
Took me from the first :—
' O nurse, let me look upon
This babe that costs so dear ;
To-morrow she will be gone :
Other mothers may keep
Their babes awake and asleep,
But I must not keep her here.'—
Whether I know or guess,
I know this not the less.

So I was sent away
That none might spy the truth :
And my childhood waxed to youth
And I left off childish play.
I never cared to play
With the village boys and girls ;
And I think they thought me proud,
I found so little to say
And kept so from the crowd :
But I had the longest curls
And I had the largest eyes
And my teeth were small like pearls ;
The girls might flout and scout me,
But the boys would hang about me
In sheepish mooning wise.

Our one-street village stood
A long mile from the town,
A mile of windy down
And bleak one-sided wood,
With not a single house.
Our town itself was small,
With just the common shops,
And throve in its small way.
Our neighbouring gentry reared
The good old-fashioned crops,
And made old-fashioned boasts
Of what John Bull would do
If Frenchman Frog appeared,
And drank old-fashioned toasts,
And made old-fashioned bows
To my Lady at the Hall.

My Lady at the Hall
Is grander than they all :
Hers is the oldest name
In all the neighbourhood ;
But the race must die with her
Though she 's a lofty dame,
For she 's unmarried still.
Poor people say she 's good
And has an open hand
As any in the land,
And she 's the comforter
Of many sick and sad ;
My nurse once said to me
That everything she had

Came of my Lady's bounty:
'Though she 's greatest in the county
She 's humble to the poor,
No beggar seeks her door
But finds help presently.
I pray both night and day
For her, and you must pray:
But she'll never feel distress
If needy folk can bless.'

I was a little maid
When here we came to live
From somewhere by the sea.
Men spoke a foreign tongue
There where we used to be
When I was merry and young,
Too young to feel afraid;
The fisher folk would give
A kind strange word to me,
There by the foreign sea:
I don't know where it was,
But I remember still
Our cottage on a hill,
And fields of flowering grass
On that fair foreign shore.

I liked my old home best,
But this was pleasant too:
So here we made our nest
And here I grew.

And now and then my Lady
In riding past our door
Would nod to Nurse and speak,
Or stoop and pat my cheek;
And I was always ready
To hold the field-gate wide
For my Lady to go through;
My Lady in her veil
So seldom put aside,
My Lady grave and pale.

I often sat to wonder
Who might my parents be,
For I knew of something under
My simple-seeming state.
Nurse never talked to me
Of mother or of father,
But watched me early and late
With kind suspicious cares:
Or not suspicious, rather
Anxious, as if she knew
Some secret I might gather
And smart for unawares.
Thus I grew.

But Nurse waxed old and grey,
Bent and weak with years.
There came a certain day
That she lay upon her bed
Shaking her palsied head,

With words she gasped to say
Which had to stay unsaid.
Then with a jerking hand
Held out so piteously
She gave a ring to me
Of gold wrought curiously,
A ring which she had worn
Since the day that I was born,
She once had said to me:
I slipped it on my finger;
Her eyes were keen to linger
On my hand that slipped it on;
Then she sighed one rattling sigh
And stared on with sightless eye:—
The one who loved me was gone.

How long I stayed alone
With the corpse I never knew,
For I fainted dead as stone:
When I came to life once more
I was down upon the floor,
With neighbours making ado
To bring me back to life.
I heard the sexton's wife
Say: 'Up, my lad, and run
To tell it at the Hall;
She was my Lady's nurse,
And done can't be undone.
I'll watch by this poor lamb.

I guess my Lady's purse
Is always open to such :
I'd run up on my crutch
A cripple as I am,'
(For cramps had vexed her much)
'Rather than this dear heart
Lack one to take her part.'

For days day after day
On my weary bed I lay
Wishing the time would pass ;
Oh, so wishing that I was
Likely to pass away :
For the one friend whom I knew
Was dead, I knew no other,
Neither father nor mother ;
And I, what should I do ?

One day the sexton's wife
Said : 'Rouse yourself, my dear :
My Lady has driven down
From the Hall into the town,
And we think she 's coming here.
Cheer up, for life is life.'

But I would not look or speak,
Would not cheer up at all.
My tears were like to fall,
So I turned round to the wall
And hid my hollow cheek

Making as if I slept,
As silent as a stone,
And no one knew I wept.
What was my Lady to me,
The grand lady from the Hall?
She might come, or stay away,
I was sick at heart that day:
The whole world seemed to be
Nothing, just nothing to me,
For aught that I could see.

Yet I listened where I lay:
A bustle came below,
A clear voice said: 'I know;
I will see her first alone,
It may be less of a shock
If she 's so weak to-day:'—
A light hand turned the lock,
A light step crossed the floor,
One sat beside my bed:
But never a word she said.

For me, my shyness grew
Each moment more and more:
So I said never a word
And neither looked nor stirred;
I think she must have heard
My heart go pit-a-pat:
Thus I lay, my Lady sat,

More than a mortal hour—
(I counted one and two
By the house-clock while I lay):
I seemed to have no power
To think of a thing to say,
Or do what I ought to do,
Or rouse myself to a choice.

At last she said: 'Margaret,
Won't you even look at me?'
A something in her voice
Forced my tears to fall at last,
Forced sobs from me thick and fast;
Something not of the past,
Yet stirring memory;
A something new, and yet
Not new, too sweet to last,
Which I never can forget.

I turned and stared at her:
Her cheek showed hollow-pale;
Her hair like mine was fair,
A wonderful fall of hair
That screened her like a veil;
But her height was statelier,
Her eyes had depth more deep;
I think they must have had
Always a something sad,
Unless they were asleep.

While I stared, my Lady took
My hand in her spare hand
Jewelled and soft and grand,
And looked with a long long look
Of hunger in my face ;
As if she tried to trace
Features she ought to know,
And half hoped, half feared, to find.
Whatever was in her mind
She heaved a sigh at last,
And began to talk to me.

'Your nurse was my dear nurse,
And her nursling's dear,' said she :
'I never knew that she was worse
Till her poor life was past'
(Here my Lady's tears dropped fast) :
'I might have been with her,
But she had no comforter.
She might have told me much
Which now I shall never know,
Never never shall know.'
She sat by me sobbing so,
And seemed so woe-begone,
That I laid one hand upon
Hers with a timid touch,
Scarce thinking what I did,
Not knowing what to say :
That moment her face was hid
In the pillow close by mine,

Her arm was flung over me,
She hugged me, sobbing so
As if her heart would break,
And kissed me where I lay.

After this she often came
To bring me fruit or wine,
Or sometimes hothouse flowers.
And at nights I lay awake
Often and often thinking
What to do for her sake.
Wet or dry it was the same:
She would come in at all hours,
Set me eating and drinking
And say I must grow strong;
At last the day seemed long
And home seemed scarcely home
If she did not come.

Well, I grew strong again:
In time of primroses,
I went to pluck them in the lane;
In time of nestling birds,
I heard them chirping round the house;
And all the herds
Were out at grass when I grew strong,
And days were waxen long,
And there was work for bees
Among the May-bush boughs,

And I had shot up tall,
And life felt after all
Pleasant, and not so long
When I grew strong.

I was going to the Hall
To be my Lady's maid:
'Her little friend,' she said to me,
'Almost her child,'
She said and smiled
Sighing painfully;
Blushing, with a second flush
As if she blushed to blush.

Friend, servant, child: just this
My standing at the Hall;
The other servants call me 'Miss,'
My Lady calls me 'Margaret,'
With her clear voice musical.
She never chides when I forget
This or that; she never chides.
Except when people come to stay,
(And that 's not often) at the Hall,
I sit with her all day
And ride out when she rides.
She sings to me and makes me sing;
Sometimes I read to her,
Sometimes we merely sit and talk.
She noticed once my ring
And made me tell its history:
That evening in our garden walk

She said she should infer
The ring had been my father's first,
Then my mother's, given for me
To the nurse who nursed
My mother in her misery,
That so quite certainly
Some one might know me, who . . .
Then she was silent, and I too.

I hate when people come:
The women speak and stare
And mean to be so civil.
This one will stroke my hair,
That one will pat my cheek
And praise my Lady's kindness,
Expecting me to speak;
I like the proud ones best
Who sit as struck with blindness,
As if I wasn't there.
But if any gentleman
Is staying at the Hall
(Though few come prying here),
My Lady seems to fear
Some downright dreadful evil,
And makes me keep my room
As closely as she can:
So I hate when people come,
It is so troublesome.
In spite of all her care,

Sometimes to keep alive
I sometimes do contrive
To get out in the grounds
For a whiff of wholesome air,
Under the rose you know:
It 's charming to break bounds,
Stolen waters are sweet,
And what 's the good of feet
If for days they mustn't go?
Give me a longer tether,
Or I may break from it.

Now I have eyes and ears
And just some little wit:
'Almost my lady's child;'
I recollect she smiled,
Sighed and blushed together;
Then her story of the ring
Sounds not improbable,
She told it me so well
It seemed the actual thing:—
Oh, keep your counsel close,
But I guess under the rose,
In long past summer weather
When the world was blossoming,
And the rose upon its thorn:
I guess not who he was
Flawed honour like a glass,
And made my life forlorn,
But my Mother, Mother, Mother,
Oh, I know her from all other.

My Lady, you might trust
Your daughter with your fame.
Trust me, I would not shame
Our honourable name,
For I have noble blood
Though I was bred in dust
And brought up in the mud.
I will not press my claim,
Just leave me where you will:
But you might trust your daughter,
For blood is thicker than water
And you're my mother still.

So my Lady holds her own
With condescending grace,
And fills her lofty place
With an untroubled face
As a queen may fill a throne.
While I could hint a tale—
(But then I am her child)—
Would make her quail;
Would set her in the dust,
Lorn with no comforter,
Her glorious hair defiled
And ashes on her cheek:
The decent world would thrust
Its finger out at her,
Not much displeased I think
To make a nine days' stir;
The decent world would sink
Its voice to speak of her.

Now this is what I mean
To do, no more, no less :
Never to speak, or show
Bare sign of what I know.
Let the blot pass unseen ;
Yea, let her never guess
I hold the tangled clue
She huddles out of view.
Friend, servant, almost child,
So be it and nothing more
On this side of the grave.
Mother, in Paradise,
You'll see with clearer eyes ;
Perhaps in this world even
When you are like to die
And face to face with Heaven
You'll drop for once the lie :
But you must drop the mask, not I.

My Lady promises
Two hundred pounds with me
Whenever I may wed
A man she can approve :
And since besides her bounty
I'm fairest in the county
(For so I've heard it said,
Though I don't vouch for this),
Her promised pounds may move
Some honest man to see
My virtues and my beauties ;

Perhaps the rising grazier,
Or temperance publican,
May claim my wifely duties.
Meanwhile I wait their leisure
And grace-bestowing pleasure,
I wait the happy man ;
But if I hold my head
And pitch my expectations
Just higher than their level,
They must fall back on patience :
I may not mean to wed,
Yet I'll be civil.

Now sometimes in a dream
My heart goes out of me
To build and scheme,
Till I sob after things that seem
So pleasant in a dream :
A home such as I see
My blessed neighbours live in
With father and with mother,
All proud of one another,
Named by one common name
From baby in the bud
To full-blown workman father ;
It 's little short of Heaven.
I'd give my gentle blood
To wash my special shame
And drown my private grudge ;
I'd toil and moil much rather

The dingiest cottage drudge
Whose mother need not blush,
Than live here like a lady
And see my Mother flush
And hear her voice unsteady
Sometimes, yet never dare
Ask to share her care.

Of course the servants sneer
Behind my back at me ;
Of course the village girls,
Who envy me my curls
And gowns and idleness,
Take comfort in a jeer ;
Of course the ladies guess
Just so much of my history
As points the emphatic stress
With which they laud my Lady ;
The gentlemen who catch
A casual glimpse of me
And turn again to see,
Their valets on the watch
To speak a word with me,
All know and sting me wild ;
Till I am almost ready
To wish that I were dead,
No faces more to see,
No more words to be said,
My Mother safe at last
Disburdened of her child,
And the past past.

'All equal before God'—
Our Rector has it so,
And sundry sleepers nod:
It may be so; I know
All are not equal here,
And when the sleepers wake
They make a difference.
'All equal in the grave'—
That shows an obvious sense:
Yet something which I crave
Not death itself brings near;
Now should death half atone
For all my past; or make
The name I bear my own?

I love my dear old Nurse
Who loved me without gains;
I love my mistress even,
Friend, Mother, what you will:
But I could almost curse
My Father for his pains;
And sometimes at my prayer
Kneeling in sight of Heaven
I almost curse him still:
Why did he set his snare
To catch at unaware
My Mother's foolish youth;
Load me with shame that's hers,
And her with something worse,
A lifelong lie for truth?

I think my mind is fixed
On one point and made up:
To accept my lot unmixed;
Never to drug the cup
But drink it by myself.
I'll not be wooed for pelf;
I'll not blot out my shame
With any man's good name;
But nameless as I stand,
My hand is my own hand,
And nameless as I came
I go to the dark land.

'All equal in the grave'—
I bide my time till then:
'All equal before God'—
To-day I feel His rod,
To-morrow He may save:
Amen.

DEVOTIONAL PIECES

DESPISED AND REJECTED

My sun has set, I dwell
In darkness as a dead man out of sight ;
And none remains, not one, that I should tell
To him mine evil plight
This bitter night.
I will make fast my door
That hollow friends may trouble me no more.

'Friend, open to Me.'—Who is this that calls ?
Nay, I am deaf as are my walls :
Cease crying, for I will not hear
Thy cry of hope or fear.
Others were dear,
Others forsook me : what art thou indeed
That I should heed
Thy lamentable need ?
Hungry should feed,
Or stranger lodge thee here ?

'Friend, My Feet bleed.
Open thy door to Me and comfort Me.'
I will not open, trouble me no more.
Go on thy way footsore,
I will not rise and open unto thee.

'Then is it nothing to thee? Open, see
Who stands to plead with thee.
Open, lest I should pass thee by, and thou
One day entreat My Face
And howl for grace,
And I be deaf as thou art now.
Open to Me.'

Then I cried out upon him: Cease,
Leave me in peace:
Fear not that I should crave
Aught thou mayst have.
Leave me in peace, yea trouble me no more,
Lest I arise and chase thee from my door.
What, shall I not be let
Alone, that thou dost vex me yet?

But all night long that voice spake urgently:
'Open to Me.'
Still harping in mine ears:
'Rise, let Me in.'
Pleading with tears:
'Open to Me that I may come to thee.'
While the dew dropped, while the dark hours were
cold:
'My Feet bleed, see My Face,
See My Hands bleed that bring thee grace,
My Heart doth bleed for thee,
Open to Me.'

So till the break of day:
Then died away
That voice, in silence as of sorrow;
Then footsteps echoing like a sigh
Passed me by,
Lingering footsteps slow to pass.
On the morrow
I saw upon the grass
Each footprint marked in blood, and on my door
The mark of blood for evermore.

LONG BARREN

Thou who didst hang upon a barren tree,
My God, for me;
  Though I till now be barren, now at length,
  Lord, give me strength
To bring forth fruit to Thee.

Thou who didst bear for me the crown of thorn,
Spitting and scorn;
  Though I till now have put forth thorns, yet now
  Strengthen me Thou
That better fruit be borne.

Thou Rose of Sharon, Cedar of broad roots,
Vine of sweet fruits,
  Thou Lily of the vale with fadeless leaf,
  Of thousands Chief,
Feed Thou my feeble shoots.

IF ONLY

If I might only love my God and die!
But now He bids me love Him and live on,
Now when the bloom of all my life is gone,
The pleasant half of life has quite gone by.
My tree of hope is lopped that spread so high;
And I forget how summer glowed and shone,
While autumn grips me with its fingers wan,
And frets me with its fitful windy sigh.
When autumn passes then must winter numb,
And winter may not pass a weary while,
But when it passes spring shall flower again:
And in that spring who weepeth now shall smile,
Yea, they shall wax who now are on the wane,
Yea, they shall sing for love when Christ shall come.

DOST THOU NOT CARE?

I love and love not: Lord, it breaks my heart
To love and not to love.
Thou veiled within Thy glory, gone apart
Into Thy shrine, which is above,
Dost thou not love me, Lord, or care
For this mine ill?—
I love thee here or there,
I will accept thy broken heart, lie still.

Lord, it was well with me in time gone by
  That cometh not again,
When I was fresh and cheerful, who but I?
  I fresh, I cheerful: worn with pain
Now, out of sight and out of heart;
  O Lord, how long?—
I watch thee as thou art,
  I will accept thy fainting heart, be strong.

'Lie still,' 'be strong,' to-day; but, Lord, to-morrow,
  What of to-morrow, Lord?
Shall there be rest from toil, be truce from sorrow,
  Be living green upon the sward
Now but a barren grave to me,
  Be joy for sorrow?—
Did I not die for thee?
  Do I not live for thee? leave Me to-morrow.

WEARY IN WELL-DOING

I WOULD have gone; God bade me stay:
  I would have worked; God bade me rest.
He broke my will from day to day,
  He read my yearnings unexpressed
    And said them nay.

Now I would stay; God bids me go:
  Now I would rest; God bids me work.
He breaks my heart tossed to and fro,
  My soul is wrung with doubts that lurk
    And vex it so.

I go, Lord, where Thou sendest me;
  Day after day I plod and moil:
But, Christ my God, when will it be
  That I may let alone my toil
    And rest with Thee?

MARTYRS' SONG

We meet in joy, though we part in sorrow;
We part to-night, but we meet to-morrow.
Be it flood or blood the path that 's trod,
All the same it leads home to God:
Be it furnace-fire voluminous,
One like God's Son will walk with us.

What are these that glow from afar,
These that lean over the golden bar,
Strong as the lion, pure as the dove,
With open arms and hearts of love?
They the blessed ones gone before,
They the blessed for evermore.
Out of great tribulation they went
Home to their home of Heaven-content;
Through flood, or blood, or furnace-fire,
To the rest that fulfils desire.

What are these that fly as a cloud,
With flashing heads and faces bowed,
In their mouths a victorious psalm,
In their hands a robe and a palm?

Welcoming angels these that shine,
Your own angel, and yours, and mine;
Who have hedged us both day and night
On the left hand and on the right,
Who have watched us both night and day
Because the devil keeps watch to slay.

Light above light, and Bliss beyond bliss,
Whom words cannot utter, lo, Who is This?
As a King with many crowns He stands,
And our names are graven upon His hands;
As a Priest, with God-uplifted eyes,
He offers for us His Sacrifice;
As the Lamb of God for sinners slain,
That we too may live He lives again;
As our Champion behold Him stand,
Strong to save us, at God's Right Hand.

God the Father give us grace
To walk in the light of Jesus' Face.
God the Son give us a part
In the hiding-place of Jesus' Heart:
God the Spirit so hold us up,
That we may drink of Jesus' cup.

Death is short and life is long;
Satan is strong, but Christ more strong.
At His Word, Who hath led us hither,
The Red Sea must part hither and thither.
At His Word, Who goes before us too,
Jordan must cleave to let us through.

Yet one pang searching and sore,
And then Heaven for evermore;
Yet one moment awful and dark,
Then safety within the Veil and the Ark;
Yet one effort by Christ His grace,
Then Christ for ever face to face.

God the Father we will adore,
In Jesus' Name, now and evermore:
God the Son we will love and thank
In this flood and on the further bank:
God the Holy Ghost we will praise,
In Jesus' Name, through endless days:
God Almighty, God Three in One,
God Almighty, God alone.

AFTER THIS THE JUDGEMENT

As eager homebound traveller to the goal,
  Or steadfast seeker on an unsearched main,
Or martyr panting for an aureole,
  My fellow-pilgrims pass me, and attain
That hidden mansion of perpetual peace
  Where keen desire and hope dwell free from pain:
That gate stands open of perennial ease;
  I view the glory till I partly long,
Yet lack the fire of love which quickens these.
  O passing Angel, speed me with a song,
A melody of heaven to reach my heart
  And rouse me to the race and make me strong;

Till in such music I take up my part
Swelling those Hallelujahs full of rest,
One, tenfold, hundredfold, with heavenly art,
Fulfilling north and south and east and west.
Thousand, ten thousandfold, innumerable,
All blent in one yet each one manifest ;
Each one distinguished and beloved as well
As if no second voice in earth or heaven
Were lifted up the Love of God to tell.
Ah, Love of God, which Thine own Self hast given
To me most poor, and made me rich in love,
Love that dost pass the tenfold seven times seven,
Draw Thou mine eyes, draw Thou my heart above,
My treasure and my heart store Thou in Thee,
Brood over me with yearnings of a dove ;
Be Husband, Brother, closest Friend to me ;
Love me as very mother loves her son,
Her sucking firstborn fondled on her knee :
Yea, more than mother loves her little one ;
For, earthly, even a mother may forget
And feel no pity for its piteous moan ;
But thou, O Love of God, remember yet,
Through the dry desert, through the waterflood
(Life, death), until the Great White Throne is set.
If now I am sick in chewing the bitter cud
Of sweet past sin, though solaced by Thy grace
And ofttimes strengthened by Thy Flesh and Blood,
How shall I then stand up before Thy face
When from Thine eyes repentance shall be hid
And utmost Justice stand in Mercy's place :

When every sin I thought or spoke or did
  Shall meet me at the inexorable bar,
And there be no man standing in the mid
  To plead for me ; while star fallen after star
With heaven and earth are like a ripened shock,
  And all time's mighty works and wonders are
Consumed as in a moment ; when no rock
  Remains to fall on me, no tree to hide,
But I stand all creation's gazing-stock
  Exposed and comfortless on every side,
Placed trembling in the final balances
  Whose poise this hour, this moment, must be tried ?—
Ah Love of God, if greater love than this
  Hath no man, that a man die for his friend,
And if such love of love Thine Own Love is,
  Plead with Thyself, with me, before the end ;
Redeem me from the irrevocable past ;
  Pitch Thou Thy Presence round me to defend ;
Yea seek with piercèd feet, yea hold me fast
  With piercèd hands whose wounds were made by love ;
Not what I am, remember what Thou wast
  When darkness hid from Thee Thy heavens above,
And sin Thy Father's Face, while thou didst drink
  The bitter cup of death, didst taste thereof
For every man ; while Thou wast nigh to sink
  Beneath the intense intolerable rod,
Grown sick of love ; not what I am, but think
  Thy Life then ransomed mine, my God, my God.

GOOD FRIDAY

Am I a stone and not a sheep
  That I can stand, O Christ, beneath Thy Cross,
  To number drop by drop Thy Blood's slow loss,
And yet not weep?

Not so those women loved
  Who with exceeding grief lamented Thee;
  Not so fallen Peter weeping bitterly;
Not so the thief was moved;

Not so the Sun and Moon
  Which hid their faces in a starless sky,
  A horror of great darkness at broad noon—
I, only I.

Yet give not o'er,
  But seek Thy sheep, true Shepherd of the flock;
  Greater than Moses, turn and look once more
And smite a rock.

THE LOWEST PLACE

Give me the lowest place: not that I dare
  Ask for that lowest place, but Thou hast died
That I might live and share
  Thy glory by Thy side.

Give me the lowest place: or if for me
  That lowest place too high, make one more low
Where I may sit and see
  My God and love Thee so.

MISCELLANEOUS POEMS, 1848–69

DEATH'S CHILL BETWEEN

(*Athenaeum*, October 14, 1848)

CHIDE not; let me breathe a little,
  For I shall not mourn him long;
Though the life-cord was so brittle,
  The love-cord was very strong.
I would wake a little space
Till I find a sleeping-place.

You can go,—I shall not weep;
  You can go unto your rest.
My heart-ache is all too deep,
  And too sore my throbbing breast.
Can sobs be, or angry tears,
Where are neither hopes nor fears?

Though with you I am alone
  And must be so everywhere,
I will make no useless moan,—
  None shall say 'She could not bear:'
While life lasts I will be strong,—
But I shall not struggle long.

Listen, listen! Everywhere
  A low voice is calling me,
And a step is on the stair,
  And one comes ye do not see.

Listen, listen! Evermore
A dim hand knocks at the door.

Hear me; he is come again,—
My own dearest is come back.
Bring him in from the cold rain;
Bring wine, and let nothing lack.
Thou and I will rest together,
Love, until the sunny weather.

I will shelter thee from harm,—
Hide thee from all heaviness.
Come to me, and keep thee warm
By my side in quietness.
I will lull thee to thy sleep
With sweet songs:—we will not weep.

Who hath talked of weeping?—Yet
There is something at my heart,
Gnawing, I would fain forget,
And an aching and a smart.
—Ah! my mother, 'tis in vain,
For he is *not* come again.

HEART'S CHILL BETWEEN

(*Athenaeum*, October 21, 1848)

I DID not chide him, though I knew
That he was false to me.
Chide the exhaling of the dew,
The ebbing of the sea,
The fading of a rosy hue,—
But not inconstancy.

Why strive for love when love is o'er?
  Why bind a restive heart?—
He never knew the pain I bore
  In saying: 'We must part;
Let us be friends and nothing more.'
  —Oh, woman's shallow art!

But it is over, it is done,—
  I hardly heed it now;
So many weary years have run
  Since then, I think not how
Things might have been,—but greet each one
  With an unruffled brow.

What time I am where others be,
  My heart seems very calm—
Stone calm; but if all go from me,
  There comes a vague alarm,
A shrinking in the memory
  From some forgotten harm.

And often through the long, long night,
  Waking when none are near,
I feel my heart beat fast with fright,
  Yet know not what I fear.
Oh how I long to see the light,
  And the sweet birds to hear!

To have the sun upon my face,
  To look up through the trees,

To walk forth in the open space
  And listen to the breeze,—
And not to dream the burial-place
  Is clogging my weak knees.

Sometimes I can nor weep nor pray,
  But am half stupefied :
And then all those who see me say
  Mine eyes are opened wide
And that my wits seem gone away —
  Ah, would that I had died !

Would I could die and be at peace,
  Or living could forget
My grief nor grows nor doth decrease,
  But ever is :—and yet
Methinks, now, that all this shall cease
  Before the sun shall set.

REPINING

(*Art and Poetry* [*The Germ*, No. 3], March 1850)

SHE sat alway thro' the long day
Spinning the weary thread away ;
And ever said in undertone :
'Come, that I be no more alone.'

From early dawn to set of sun
Working, her task was still undone ;
And the long thread seemed to increase
Even while she spun and did not cease.

She heard the gentle turtle-dove
Tell to its mate a tale of love ;
She saw the glancing swallows fly,
Ever a social company ;
She knew each bird upon its nest
Had cheering songs to bring it rest ;
None lived alone save only she ;—
The wheel went round more wearily ;
She wept and said in undertone :
'Come, that I be no more alone.'

Day followed day, and still she sighed
For love, and was not satisfied ;
Until one night, when the moonlight
Turned all the trees to silver white,
She heard, what ne'er she heard before,
A steady hand undo the door.
The nightingale since set of sun
Her throbbing music had not done,
And she had listened silently ;
But now the wind had changed, and she
Heard the sweet song no more, but heard
Beside her bed a whispered word :
'Damsel, rise up ; be not afraid ;
For I am come at last,' it said.

She trembled, tho' the voice was mild ;
She trembled like a frightened child ;—
Till she looked up, and then she saw
The unknown speaker without awe.

He seemed a fair young man, his eyes
Beaming with serious charities;
His cheek was white but hardly pale;
And a dim glory like a veil
Hovered about his head, and shone
Thro' the whole room till night was gone.

So her fear fled; and then she said,
Leaning upon her quiet bed:
'Now thou art come, I prithee stay,
That I may see thee in the day,
And learn to know thy voice, and hear
It evermore calling me near.'

He answered: 'Rise, and follow me.'
But she looked upwards wonderingly:
'And whither would'st thou go, friend? stay
Until the dawning of the day.'
But he said: 'The wind ceaseth, Maid;
Of chill nor damp be thou afraid.'

She bound her hair up from the floor,
And passed in silence from the door.

So they went forth together, he
Helping her forward tenderly.
The hedges bowed beneath his hand;
Forth from the streams came the dry land
As they passed over; evermore
The pallid moonbeams shone before;

And the wind hushed, and nothing stirred;
Not even a solitary bird,
Scared by their footsteps, fluttered by
Where aspen-trees stood steadily.

As they went on, at length a sound
Came trembling on the air around;
The undistinguishable hum
Of life, voices that go and come
Of busy men, and the child's sweet
High laugh, and noise of trampling feet.

Then he said: 'Wilt thou go and see?'
And she made answer joyfully:
'The noise of life, of human life,
Of dear communion without strife,
Of converse held 'twixt friend and friend;
Is it not here our path shall end?'
He led her on a little way
Until they reached a hillock: 'Stay.'

It was a village in a plain.
High mountains screened it from the rain
And stormy wind; and nigh at hand
A bubbling streamlet flowed, o'er sand
Pebbly and fine, and sent life up
Green succous stalk and flower-cup.

Gradually, day's harbinger,
A chilly wind began to stir.

It seemed a gentle powerless breeze
That scarcely rustled thro' the trees;
And yet it touched the mountain's head
And the paths man might never tread.
But hearken: in the quiet weather
Do all the streams flow down together?—

No, 'tis a sound more terrible
Than tho' a thousand rivers fell.
The everlasting ice and snow
Were loosened then, but not to flow;—
With a loud crash like solid thunder
The avalanche came, burying under
The village; turning life and breath
And rest and joy and plans to death.

'Oh! let us fly, for pity fly;
Let us go hence, friend, thou and I.
There must be many regions yet
Where these things make not desolate.'
He looked upon her seriously;
Then said: 'Arise and follow me.'
The path that lay before them was
Nigh covered over with long grass;
And many slimy things and slow
Trailed on between the roots below.
The moon looked dimmer than before;
And shadowy cloudlets floating o'er
Its face sometimes quite hid its light,
And filled the skies with deeper night.

At last, as they went on, the noise
Was heard of the sea's mighty voice ;
And soon the ocean could be seen
In its long restlessness serene.
Upon its breast a vessel rode
That drowsily appeared to nod
As the great billows rose and fell,
And swelled to sink, and sank to swell.

Meanwhile the strong wind had come forth
From the chill regions of the North,
The mighty wind invisible.
And the low waves began to swell ;
And the sky darkened overhead ;
And the moon once looked forth, then fled
Behind dark clouds ; while here and there
The lightning shone out in the air ;
And the approaching thunder rolled
With angry pealings manifold.
How many vows were made, and prayers
That in safe times were cold and scarce.
Still all availed not ; and at length
The waves arose in all their strength,
And fought against the ship, and filled
The ship. Then were the clouds unsealed,
And the rain hurried forth, and beat
On every side and over it.

Some clung together, and some kept
A long stern silence, and some wept.

Many half-crazed looked on in wonder
As the strong timbers rent asunder;
Friends forgot friends, foes fled to foes;—
And still the water rose and rose.

'Ah woe is me! Whom I have seen
Are now as tho' they had not been.
In the earth there is room for birth,
And there are graves enough in earth;
Why should the cold sea, tempest-torn,
Bury those whom it hath not borne?'

He answered not, and they went on.
The glory of the heavens was gone;
The moon gleamed not nor any star;
Cold winds were rustling near and far,
And from the trees the dry leaves fell
With a sad sound unspeakable.
The air was cold; till from the South
A gust blew hot, like sudden drouth,
Into their faces; and a light
Glowing and red, shone thro' the night.

A mighty city full of flame
And death and sounds without a name.
Amid the black and blinding smoke,
The people, as one man, awoke.
Oh! happy they who yesterday
On the long journey went away;
Whose pallid lips, smiling and chill,
While the flames scorch them smile on still;

Who murmur not; who tremble not
When the bier crackles fiery hot;
Who, dying, said in love's increase:
'Lord, let thy servant part in peace.'

Those in the town could see and hear
A shaded river flowing near;
The broad deep bed could hardly hold
Its plenteous waters calm and cold.
Was flame-wrapped all the city wall,
The city gates were flame-wrapped all.

What was man's strength, what puissance then?
Women were mighty as strong men.
Some knelt in prayer, believing still,
Resigned unto a righteous will,
Bowing beneath the chastening rod,
Lost to the world, but found of God.
Some prayed for friend, for child, for wife;
Some prayed for faith; some prayed for life;
While some, proud even in death, hope gone,
Steadfast and still, stood looking on.

'Death—death—oh! let us fly from death;
Where'er we go it followeth;
All these are dead; and we alone
Remain to weep for what is gone.
What is this thing? thus hurriedly
To pass into eternity;
To leave the earth so full of mirth;
To lose the profit of our birth;

To die and be no more ; to cease,
Having numbness that is not peace.
Let us go hence ; and, even if thus
Death everywhere must go with us,
Let us not see the change, but see
Those who have been or still shall be.'

He sighed and they went on together
Beneath their feet did the grass wither ;
Across the heaven high overhead
Dark misty clouds floated and fled ;
And in their bosom was the thunder,
And angry lightnings flashed out under,
Forked and red and menacing ;
Far off the wind was muttering ;
It seemed to tell, not understood,
Strange secrets to the listening wood.

Upon its wings it bore the scent
Of blood of a great armament :
Then saw they how on either side
Fields were down-trodden far and wide.
That morning at the break of day
Two nations had gone forth to slay.

As a man soweth so he reaps.
The field was full of bleeding heaps ;
Ghastly corpses of men and horses
That met death at a thousand sources ;

Cold limbs and putrefying flesh ;
Long love-locks clotted to a mesh
That stifled ; stiffened mouths beneath
Staring eyes that had looked on death.

But these were dead : these felt no more
The anguish of the wounds they bore.
Behold, they shall not sigh again,
Nor justly fear, nor hope in vain.
What if none wept above them ?—is
The sleeper less at rest for this ?
Is not the young child's slumber sweet
When no man watcheth over it ?
These had deep calm ; but all around
There was a deadly smothered sound,
The choking cry of agony
From wounded men who could not die ;
Who watched the black wing of the raven
Rise like a cloud 'twixt them and heaven,
And in the distance flying fast
Beheld the eagle come at last.

She knelt down in her agony :
'O Lord, it is enough,' said she :
'My heart's prayer putteth me to shame ;
Let me return to whence I came.
Thou who for love's sake didst reprove,
Forgive me for the sake of love.'

SIT DOWN IN THE LOWEST ROOM

(*Macmillan's Magazine*, March 1864.)

LIKE flowers sequestered from the sun
  And wind of summer, day by day
I dwindled paler, whilst my hair
    Showed the first tinge of grey

'Oh what is life, that we should live ?
  Or what is death, that we must die ?
A bursting bubble is our life :
    I also, what am I ?'

'What is your grief ? now tell me, sweet,
  That I may grieve,' my sister said ;
And stayed a white embroidering hand
    And raised a golden head :

Her tresses showed a richer mass,
  Her eyes looked softer than my own,
Her figure had a statelier height,
    Her voice a tenderer tone.

'Some must be second and not first ;
  All cannot be the first of all :
Is not this, too, but vanity ?
    I stumble like to fall.

'So yesterday I read the acts
Of Hector and each clangorous king
With wrathful great Æacides:—
Old Homer leaves a sting.'

The comely face looked up again,
The deft hand lingered on the thread:
'Sweet, tell me what is Homer's sting,
Old Homer's sting?' she said.

'He stirs my sluggish pulse like wine,
He melts me like the wind of spice,
Strong as strong Ajax' red right hand,
And grand like Juno's eyes.

'I cannot melt the sons of men,
I cannot fire and tempest-toss:—
Besides, those days were golden days,
Whilst these are days of dross.'

She laughed a feminine low laugh,
Yet did not stay her dexterous hand:
'Now tell me of those days,' she said,
'When time ran golden sand.'

'Then men were men of might and right,
Sheer might, at least, and weighty swords;
Then men in open blood and fire,
Bore witness to their words,

‘Crest-rearing kings with whistling spears;
But if these shivered in the shock
They wrenched up hundred-rooted trees,
Or hurled the effacing rock.

‘Then hand to hand, then foot to foot,
Stern to the death-grip grappling then,
Who ever thought of gunpowder
Amongst these men of men?

‘They knew whose hand struck home the death,
They knew who broke but would not bend,
Could venerate an equal foe
And scorn a laggard friend.

‘Calm in the utmost stress of doom,
Devout toward adverse powers above,
They hated with intenser hate
And loved with fuller love.

‘Then heavenly beauty could allay
As heavenly beauty stirred the strife:
By them a slave was worshipped more
Than is by us a wife.’

She laughed again, my sister laughed,
Made answer o’er the laboured cloth:
‘I rather would be one of us
Than wife, or slave, or both.’

'Oh better then be slave or wife
  Than fritter now blank life away:
Then night had holiness of night,
  And day was sacred day.

'The princess laboured at her loom,
  Mistress and handmaiden alike;
Beneath their needles grew the field
  With warriors armed to strike;

'Or, look again, dim Dian's face
  Gleamed perfect through the attendant night;
Were such not better than those holes
  Amid that waste of white?

'A shame it is, our aimless life:
  I rather from my heart would feed
From silver dish in gilded stall
  With wheat and wine the steed—

'The faithful steed that bore my lord
  In safety through the hostile land,
The faithful steed that arched his neck
  To fondle with my hand.'

Her needle erred; a moment's pause,
  A moment's patience, all was well.
Then she: 'But just suppose the horse,
  Suppose the rider fell?

'Then captive in an alien house,
  Hungering on exile's bitter bread,—
They happy, they who won the lot
    Of sacrifice,' she said.

Speaking she faltered, while her look
  Showed forth her passion like a glass:
With hand suspended, kindling eye,
    Flushed cheek, how fair she was!

'Ah well, be those the days of dross;
  This, if you will, the age of gold:
Yet had those days a spark of warmth,
    While these are somewhat cold—

'Are somewhat mean and cold and slow,
  Are stunted from heroic growth:
We gain but little when we prove
    The worthlessness of both.'

'But life is in our hands,' she said:
  'In our own hands for gain or loss:
Shall not the Sevenfold Sacred Fire
    Suffice to purge our dross?

'Too short a century of dreams,
  One day of work sufficient length:
Why should not you, why should not I
    Attain heroic strength?

'Our life is given us as a blank;
Ourselves must make it blest or curst:
Who dooms me I shall only be
The second, not the first?

'Learn from old Homer, if you will,
Such wisdom as his Books have said:
In one the acts of Ajax shine,
In one of Diomed.

'Honoured all heroes whose high deeds
Thro' life till death enlarge their span:
Only Achilles in his rage
And sloth is less than man.'

'Achilles only less than man?
He less than man who, half a god,
Discomfited all Greece with rest,
Cowed Ilion with a nod?

'He offered vengeance, lifelong grief
To one dear ghost, uncounted price:
Beasts, Trojans, adverse gods, himself,
Heaped up the sacrifice.

'Self-immolated to his friend,
Shrined in world's wonder, Homer's page,
Is this the man, the less than men,
Of this degenerate age?'

' Gross from his acorns, tusky boar
  Does memorable acts like his ;
So for her snared offended young
    Bleeds the swart lioness.'

But here she paused ; our eyes had met,
  And I was whitening with the jeer ;
She rose : ' I went too far,' she said ;
    Spoke low : ' Forgive me, dear.

' To me our days seem pleasant days,
  Our home a haven of pure content ;
Forgive me if I said too much,
    So much more than I meant.

' Homer, tho' greater than his gods,
  With rough-hewn virtues was sufficed
And rough-hewn men : but what are such
    To us who learn of Christ ? '

The much-moved pathos of her voice,
  Her almost tearful eyes, her cheek
Grown pale, confessed the strength of love
    Which only made her speak :

For mild she was, of few soft words,
  Most gentle, easy to be led,
Content to listen when I spoke
    And reverence what I said ;

I elder sister by six years;
  Not half so glad, or wise, or good:
Her words rebuked my secret self
    And shamed me where I stood.

She never guessed her words reproved
  A silent envy nursed within,
A selfish, souring discontent
    Pride-born, the devil's sin.

I smiled, half bitter, half in jest:
  'The wisest man of all the wise
Left for his summary of life
    "Vanity of vanities."

'Beneath the sun there 's nothing new:
  Men flow, men ebb, mankind flows on:
If I am wearied of my life,
    Why so was Solomon.

'Vanity of vanities he preached
  Of all he found, of all he sought:
Vanity of vanities, the gist
    Of all the words he taught.

'This in the wisdom of the world,
  In Homer's page, in all, we find:
As the sea is not filled, so yearns
    Man's universal mind.

'This Homer felt, who gave his men
  With glory but a transient state :
His very Jove could not reverse
    Irrevocable fate.

'Uncertain all their lot save this—
  Who wins must lose, who lives must die :
All trodden out into the dark
    Alike, all vanity.'

She scarcely answered when I paused,
  But rather to herself said : 'One
Is here,' low-voiced and loving, 'Yea,
    Greater than Solomon.'

So both were silent, she and I :
  She laid her work aside, and went
Into the garden-walks, like spring,
    All gracious with content,

A little graver than her wont,
  Because her words had fretted me ;
Not warbling quite her merriest tune
    Bird-like from tree to tree.

I chose a book to read and dream :
  Yet all the while with furtive eyes
Marked how she made her choice of flowers
    Intuitively wise,

And ranged them with instinctive taste
  Which all my books had failed to teach;
Fresh rose herself, and daintier
    Than blossom of the peach.

By birthright higher than myself,
  Tho' nestling of the self-same nest:
No fault of hers, no fault of mine,
    But stubborn to digest.

I watched her, till my book unmarked
  Slid noiseless to the velvet floor;
Till all the opulent summer-world
    Looked poorer than before.

Just then her busy fingers ceased,
  Her fluttered colour went and came;
I knew whose step was on the walk,
    Whose voice would name her name.

* * * * * * * *

Well, twenty years have passed since then:
  My sister now, a stately wife
Still fair, looks back in peace and sees
    The longer half of life—

The longer half of prosperous life,
  With little grief, or fear, or fret:
She loved, and, loving long ago,
    Is loved and loving yet.

A husband honourable, brave,
  Is her main wealth in all the world :
And next to him one like herself,
    One daughter golden-curled ;

Fair image of her own fair youth,
  As beautiful and as serene,
With almost such another love
    As her own love has been.

Yet, tho' of world-wide charity,
  And in her home most tender dove,
Her treasure and her heart are stored
    In the home-land of love :

She thrives, God's blessed husbandry ;
  She like a vine is full of fruit ;
Her passion-flower climbs up toward heaven
    Tho' earth still binds its root.

I sit and watch my sister's face :
  How little altered since the hours
When she, a kind, light-hearted girl,
    Gathered her garden flowers ;

Her song just mellowed by regret
  For having teased me with her talk ;
Then all-forgetful as she heard
    One step upon the walk.

While I? I sat alone and watched
  My lot in life, to live alone,
In mine own world of interests,
    Much felt but little shown.

Not to be first: how hard to learn
  That lifelong lesson of the past;
Line graven on line and stroke on stroke;
    But, thank God, learned at last.

So now in patience I possess
  My soul year after tedious year,
Content to take the lowest place,
    The place assigned me here.

Yet sometimes, when I feel my strength
  Most weak, and life most burdensome,
I lift mine eyes up to the hills
    From whence my help shall come:

Yea, sometimes still I lift my heart
  To the Archangelic trumpet-burst,
When all deep secrets shall be shown,
    And many last be first.

MY FRIEND

(*Macmillan's Magazine*, Dec. 1864.)

Two days ago with dancing glancing hair,
  With living lips and eyes:
  Now pale, dumb, blind, she lies;
So pale, yet still so fair.

We have not left her yet, not yet alone;
But soon must leave her where
She will not miss our care,
Bone of our bone.

Weep not; O friends, we should not weep:
Our friend of friends lies full of rest;
No sorrow rankles in her breast,
Fallen fast asleep.

She sleeps below,
She wakes and laughs above:
To-day, as she walked, let us walk in love;
To-morrow follow so.

LAST NIGHT

(*Macmillan's Magazine*, May 1865.)

WHERE were you last night? I watched at the gate;
I went down early, I stayed down late.
Were you snug at home, I should like to know,
Or were you in the coppice wheedling Kate?

She's a fine girl, with a fine clear skin;
Easy to woo, perhaps not hard to win.
Speak up like a man and tell me the truth:
I'm not one to grow downhearted and thin.

If you love her best speak up like a man ;
It 's not I will stand in the light of your plan :
  Some girls might cry and scold you a bit,
And say they couldn't bear it ; but I can.

Love was pleasant enough, and the days went fast ;
Pleasant while it lasted, but it needn't last ;
  Awhile on the wax, and awhile on the wane,
Now dropped away into the past.

Was it pleasant to you ? To me it was :
Now clean gone as an image from glass,
  As a goodly rainbow that fades away,
As dew that steams upward from the grass,

As the first spring day, or the last summer day,
As the sunset flush that leaves heaven grey,
  As a flame burnt out for lack of oil,
Which no pains relight or ever may.

Good luck to Kate and good luck to you .
I guess she'll be kind when you come to woo.
  I wish her a pretty face that will last,
I wish her a husband steady and true.

Hate you ? not I, my very good friend ;
All things begin and all have an end.
  But let broken be broken ; I put no faith
In quacks who set up to patch and mend.

Just my love and one word to Kate:
Not to let time slip if she means to mate;—
For even such a thing has been known
As to miss the chance while we weigh and wait.

CONSIDER

(*Macmillan's Magazine*, Jan. 1866.)

CONSIDER
The lilies of the field whose bloom is brief:—
We are as they;
Like them we fade away,
As doth a leaf.

Consider
The sparrows of the air of small account:
Our God doth view
Whether they fall or mount,—
He guards us too.

Consider
The lilies that do neither spin nor toil,
Yet are most fair:—
What profits all this care
And all this coil?

Consider
The birds that have no barn nor harvest-weeks;
God gives them food:—
Much more our Father seeks
To do us good.

HELEN GREY

(*Macmillan's Magazine,* March 1866.)

BECAUSE one loves you, Helen Grey,
  Is that a reason you should pout,
  And like a March wind veer about,
And frown, and say your shrewish say ?
Don't strain the cord until it snaps,
  Don't split the sound heart with your wedge,
  Don't cut your fingers with the edge
Of your keen wit ; you may, perhaps.

Because you're handsome, Helen Grey,
  Is that a reason to be proud ?
  Your eyes are bold, your laugh is loud,
Your steps go mincing on their way ;
But so you miss that modest charm
  Which is the surest charm of all :
  Take heed, you yet may trip and fall,
And no man care to stretch his arm.

Stoop from your cold height, Helen Grey,
  Come down, and take a lowlier place,
  Come down, to fill it now with grace ;
Come down you must perforce some day :
For years cannot be kept at bay,
  And fading years will make you old ;
  Then in their turn will men seem cold,
When you yourself are nipped and grey.

261

BY THE WATERS OF BABYLON

B. C. 570

(*Macmillan's Magazine*, October 1866.)

HERE where I dwell I waste to skin and bone;
The curse is come upon me, and I waste
In penal torment powerless to atone.
The curse is come on me, which makes no haste
And doth not tarry, crushing both the proud
Hard man and him the sinner double-faced.
Look not upon me, for my soul is bowed
Within me, as my body in this mire;
My soul crawls dumb-struck, sore-bested and cowed.
As Sodom and Gomorrah scourged by fire,
As Jericho before God's trumpet-peal,
So we the elect ones perish in His ire.
Vainly we gird on sackcloth, vainly kneel
With famished faces toward Jerusalem:
His heart is shut against us not to feel,
His ears against our cry He shutteth them,
His hand He shorteneth that He will not save,
His law is loud against us to condemn:
And we, as unclean bodies in the grave
Inheriting corruption and the dark,
Are outcast from His presence which we crave.
Our Mercy hath departed from His Ark,
Our Glory hath departed from His rest,
Our Shield hath left us naked as a mark
Unto all pitiless eyes made manifest.

Our very Father hath forsaken us,
Our God hath cast us from Him: we oppress'd
Unto our foes are even marvellous,
A hissing and a butt for pointing hands,
Whilst God Almighty hunts and grinds us thus;
For He hath scattered us in alien lands, 31
Our priests, our princes, our anointed king,
And bound us hand and foot with brazen bands.
Here while I sit my painful heart takes wing
Home to the home-land I must see no more,
Where milk and honey flow, where waters spring
And fail not, where I dwelt in days of yore
Under my fig-tree and my fruitful vine,
There where my parents dwelt at ease before:
Now strangers press the olives that are mine, 40
Reap all the corners of my harvest-field,
And make their fat hearts wanton with my wine;
To them my trees, to them my gardens yield
Their sweets and spices and their tender green,
O'er them in noontide heat outspread their shield.
Yet these are they whose fathers had not been
Housed with my dogs, whom hip and thigh we smote
And with their blood washed their pollutions clean,
Purging the land which spewed them from its throat; 49
Their daughters took we for a pleasant prey,
Choice tender ones on whom the fathers doat.
Now they in turn have led our own away;

Our daughters and our sisters and our wives
Sore weeping as they weep who curse the day,
To live, remote from help, dishonoured lives,
Soothing their drunken masters with a song,
Or dancing in their golden tinkling gyves:
Accurst if they remember through the long
Estrangement of their exile, twice accursed
If they forget and join the accursèd throng.
How doth my heart that is so wrung not burst
When I remember that my way was plain,
And that God's candle lit me at the first,
Whilst now I grope in darkness, grope in vain,
Desiring but to find Him Who is lost,
To find Him once again, but once again.
His wrath came on us to the uttermost,
His covenanted and most righteous wrath:
Yet this is He of Whom we made our boast,
Who lit the Fiery Pillar in our path,
Who swept the Red Sea dry before our feet,
Who in His jealousy smote kings, and hath
Sworn once to David: One shall fill thy seat
Born of thy body, as the sun and moon
'Stablished for aye in sovereignty complete.
O Lord, remember David, and that soon.
The Glory hath departed, Ichabod!
Yet now, before our sun grow dark at noon,
Before we come to nought beneath Thy rod,
Before we go down quick into the pit,
Remember us for good, O God, our God:—
Thy Name will I remember, praising it,

Though Thou forget me, though Thou hide Thy face,
And blot me from the Book which Thou hast writ;
Thy Name will I remember in my praise
And call to mind Thy faithfulness of old,
Though as a weaver Thou cut off my days,
And end me as a tale ends that is told.

SEASONS

(*Macmillan's Magazine*, Dec. 1866.)

OH the cheerful Budding-time!
When thorn-hedges turn to green,
When new leaves of elm and lime
Cleave and shed their winter screen;
Tender lambs are born and 'baa',
North wind finds no snow to bring,
Vigorous Nature laughs 'Ha, ha',
In the miracle of spring.

Oh the gorgeous Blossom-days!
When broad flag-flowers drink and blow,
In and out in summer-blaze
Dragon-flies flash to and fro;
Ashen branches hang out keys,
Oaks put forth the rosy shoot,
Wandering herds wax sleek at ease,
Lovely blossoms end in fruit.

Oh the shouting Harvest-weeks !
  Mother earth grown fat with sheaves
Thrifty gleaner finds who seeks ;
  Russet-golden pomp of leaves
Crowns the woods, to fall at length ;
  Bracing winds are felt to stir,
Ocean gathers up her strength,
  Beasts renew their dwindled fur.

Oh the starving Winter-lapse !
  Ice-bound, hunger-pinched and dim ;
Dormant roots recall their saps,
  Empty nests show black and grim,
Short-lived sunshine gives no heat,
  Undue buds are nipped by frost,
Snow sets forth a winding-sheet,
  And all hope of life seems lost.

MOTHER COUNTRY

(*Macmillan's Magazine,* March 1868.)

Oh what is that country
  And where can it be,
Not mine own country,
  But dearer far to me ?
Yet mine own country,
  If I one day may see
Its spices and cedars,
  Its gold and ivory.

As I lie dreaming
  It rises, that land :
There rises before me
  Its green golden strand,
With its bowing cedars
  And its shining sand ;
It sparkles and flashes
  Like a shaken brand.

Do angels lean nearer
  While I lie and long ?
I see their soft plumage
  And catch their windy song,
Like the rise of a high tide
  Sweeping full and strong ;
I mark the outskirts
  Of their reverend throng.

Oh what is a king here,
  Or what is a boor ?
Here all starve together,
  All dwarfed and poor ;
Here Death's hand knocketh
  At door after door,
He thins the dancers
  From the festal floor.

Oh what is a handmaid,
  Or what is a queen ?
All must lie down together
  Where the turf is green,

The foulest face hidden,
  The fairest not seen;
Gone as if never,
  They had breathed or been.

Gone from sweet sunshine
  Underneath the sod,
Turned from warm flesh and blood
  To senseless clod,
Gone as if never
  They had toiled or trod,
Gone out of sight of all
  Except our God.

Shut into silence
  From the accustomed song,
Shut into solitude
  From all earth's throng,
Run down tho' swift of foot,
  Thrust down tho' strong;
Life made an end of
  Seemed it short or long.

Life made an end of,
  Life but just begun,
Life finished yesterday,
  Its last sand run;
Life new-born with the morrow,
  Fresh as the sun:
While done is done for ever;
  Undone, undone.

And if that life is life,
  This is but a breath,
The passage of a dream
  And the shadow of death ;
But a vain shadow
  If one considereth ;
Vanity of vanities,
  As the Preacher saith.

A SMILE AND A SIGH

(*Macmillan's Magazine*, May 1868.)

A SMILE because the nights are short !
  And every morning brings such pleasure
Of sweet love-making, harmless sport :
  Love, that makes and finds its treasure ;
  Love, treasure without measure.

A sigh because the days are long !
  Long long these days that pass in sighing,
A burden saddens every song :
  While time lags who should be flying,
  We live who would be dying.

DEAD HOPE

(*Macmillan's Magazine*, May 1868.)

HOPE new born one pleasant morn
  Died at even ;
Hope dead lives nevermore.
  No, not in heaven.

If his shroud were but a cloud
  To weep itself away ;
Or were he buried underground
  To sprout some day !
But dead and gone is dead and gone
  Vainly wept upon.

Nought we place above his face
  To mark the spot,
But it shows a barren place
  In our lot.
Hope has birth no more on earth
  Morn or even ;
Hope dead lives nevermore,
  No, not in heaven.

AUTUMN VIOLETS

(*Macmillan's Magazine*, November 1868.)

KEEP love for youth, and violets for the spring :
Or if these bloom when worn-out autumn grieves,
Let them lie hid in double shade of leaves,
Their own, and others dropped down withering ;
For violets suit when home birds build and sing,
Not when the outbound bird a passage cleaves ;
Not with the stubble of mown harvest sheaves,
But when the green world buds to blossoming.
Keep violets for the spring, and love for youth,
Love that should dwell with beauty, mirth, and hope :

Or if a later sadder love be born,
Let this not look for grace beyond its scope,
But give itself, nor plead for answering truth—
A grateful Ruth tho' gleaning scanty corn.

'THEY DESIRE A BETTER COUNTRY'

(*Macmillan's Magazine*, March 1869.)

I

I WOULD not if I could undo my past,
  Tho' for its sake my future is a blank;
  My past, for which I have myself to thank
For all its faults and follies first and last.
I would not cast anew the lot once cast,
  Or launch a second ship for one that sank,
  Or drug with sweets the bitterness I drank,
Or break by feasting my perpetual fast.
I would not if I could: for much more dear
  Is one remembrance than a hundred joys,
    More than a thousand hopes in jubilee;
  Dearer the music of one tearful voice
    That unforgotten calls and calls to me,
'Follow me here, rise up, and follow here.'

II

What seekest thou far in the unknown land?
  In hope I follow joy gone on before,
  In hope and fear persistent more and more,
As the dry desert lengthens out its sand.

Whilst day and night I carry in my hand
The golden key to ope the golden door
Of golden home ; yet mine eye weepeth sore
For the long journey that must make no stand.
And who is this that veiled doth walk with thee ?
Lo, this is Love that walketh at my right ;
One exile holds us both, and we are bound
To selfsame home-joys in the land of light.
Weeping thou walkest with him ; weepeth he ?—
Some sobbing weep, some weep and make no
sound.

III

A dimness of a glory glimmers here
Thro' veils and distance from the space remote,
A faintest far vibration of a note
Reaches to us and seems to bring us near,
Causing our face to glow with braver cheer,
Making the serried mist to stand afloat,
Subduing languor with an antidote,
And strengthening love almost to cast out fear,
Till for one moment golden city walls
Rise looming on us, golden walls of home,
Light of our eyes until the darkness falls ;
Then thro' the outer darkness burdensome
I hear again the tender voice that calls,
'Follow me hither, follow, rise, and come.'

THE OFFERING OF THE NEW LAW, THE ONE OBLATION ONCE OFFERED

(*Lyra Eucharistica*, 1863.)

Once I thought to sit so high
In the Palace of the sky;
Now, I thank God for His Grace,
If I may fill the lowest place.

Once I thought to scale so soon
Heights above the changing moon;
Now, I thank God for delay—
To-day, it yet is called to-day.

While I stumble, halt and blind,
Lo! He waiteth to be kind;
Bless me soon, or bless me slow,
Except He bless, I let not go.

Once for earth I laid my plan,
Once I leaned on strength of man,
When my hope was swept aside,
I stayed my broken heart on pride:

Broken reed hath pierced my hand;
Fell my house I built on sand;
Roofless, wounded, maimed by sin,
Fightings without and fears within:

Yet, a tree, He feeds my root;
Yet, a branch, He prunes for fruit;
Yet, a sheep, these eves and morns,
He seeks for me among the thorns.

With Thine Image stamped of old,
Find Thy coin more choice than gold;
Known to Thee by name, recall
To Thee Thy home-sick prodigal.

Sacrifice and Offering
None there is that I can bring,
None, save what is Thine alone:
I bring Thee, Lord, but of Thine Own—

Broken Body, Blood Outpoured,
These I bring, my God, my Lord;
Wine of Life, and Living Bread,
With these for me Thy Board is spread.

CONFERENCE BETWEEN CHRIST, THE SAINTS, AND THE SOUL

(*Lyra Eucharistica*, 1863.)

I AM pale with sick desire,
  For my heart is far away
From this world's fitful fire
  And this world's waning day;
In a dream it overleaps
  A world of tedious ills
To where the sunshine sleeps
  On th' everlasting hills.
  Say the Saints—There Angels ease us
    Glorified and white.
  They say—We rest in Jesus,
    Where is not day nor night.

My Soul saith—I have sought
  For a home that is not gained,
I have spent yet nothing bought,
  Have laboured but not attained;
My pride strove to rise and grow,
  And hath but dwindled down;
My love sought love, and lo!
  Hath not attained its crown.
  Say the Saints—Fresh Souls increase us,
    None languish nor recede.
  They say—We love our Jesus,
    And He loves us indeed.

I cannot rise above,
  I cannot rest beneath,
I cannot find out Love,
  Nor escape from Death;
Dear hopes and joys gone by
  Still mock me with a name;
My best belovèd die
  And I cannot die with them.
  Say the Saints—No deaths decrease us,
    Where our rest is glorious.
  They say—We live in Jesus,
    Who once dièd for us.

Oh, my Soul, she beats her wings
  And pants to fly away
Up to immortal Things
  In the Heavenly day:

Yet she flags and almost faints;
Can such be meant for me?
Come and see—say the Saints.
Saith Jesus—Come and see.
Say the Saints—His Pleasures please us
Before God and the Lamb.
Come and taste My Sweets—saith Jesus—
Be with Me where I am. 48

COME UNTO ME

(*Lyra Eucharistica*, second edition, 1864.)

Oh, for the time gone by, when thought of Christ
Made His Yoke easy and His Burden light;
When my heart stirred within me at the sight
Of Altar spread for awful Eucharist;
When all my hopes His Promises sufficed,
When my Soul watched for Him by day, by night,
When my lamp lightened and my robe was white,
And all seemed loss, except the Pearl unpriced.
Yet, since He calls me still with tender Call,
Since He remembers Whom I half forgot,
I even will run my race and bear my lot:
For Faith the walls of Jericho cast down,
And Hope to whoso runs holds forth a Crown,
And Love is Christ, and Christ is All in all.

JESUS, DO I LOVE THEE ?

(*Lyra Eucharistica*, second edition, 1864.)

Jesus, do I love Thee ?
Thou art far above me,
Seated out of sight
Hid in Heavenly Light
Of most highest height.
Martyred hosts implore Thee,
Seraphs fall before Thee,
Angels and Archangels,
Cherub throngs adore Thee ;
Blessed She that bore Thee !
All the Saints approve Thee,
All the Virgins love Thee.
I show as a blot
Blood hath cleansed not,
As a barren spot
In Thy fruitful lot.
I, fig-tree fruit-unbearing ;
Thou, righteous Judge unsparing :
What canst Thou do more to me
That shall not more undo me ?
Thy Justice hath a sound—
Why cumbereth it the ground ?
Thy Love with stirrings stronger
Pleads—Give it one year longer.
Thou giv'st me time : but who
Save Thou shall give me dew ;

Shall feed my root with Blood,
And stir my sap for good?
Oh, by Thy Gifts that shame me,
Give more lest they condemn me:
Good Lord, I ask much of Thee,
But most I ask to love Thee;
Kind Lord, be mindful of me,
Love me, and make me love Thee.

I KNOW YOU NOT

(*Lyra Messianica,* 1864.)

O Christ, the Vine with living Fruit,
The twelvefold-fruited Tree of Life,
The Balm in Gilead after strife,
The valley Lily and the Rose;
Stronger than Lebanon, Thou Root;
Sweeter than clustered grapes, Thou Vine;
O Best, Thou Vineyard of red wine,
Keeping thy best wine till the close.

Pearl of great price Thyself alone,
And ruddier than the ruby Thou;
Most precious lightning Jasper stone,
Head of the corner spurned before:
Fair Gate of pearl, Thyself the Door;
Clear golden Street, Thyself the Way;
By Thee we journey toward Thee now,
Through Thee shall enter Heaven one day.

I thirst for Thee, full fount and flood;
My heart calls Thine, as deep to deep:
Dost Thou forget Thy sweat and pain,
Thy provocation on the Cross?
Heart-pierced for me, vouchsafe to keep
The purchase of Thy lavished Blood:
The gain is Thine, Lord, if I gain;
Or if I lose, Thine own the loss.

At midnight (saith the Parable)
A cry was made, the Bridegroom came;
Those who were ready entered in:
The rest, shut out in death and shame,
Strove all too late that Feast to win,
Their die was cast, and fixed their lot;
A gulf divided Heaven from Hell;
The Bridegroom said—I know you not.

But Who is this that shuts the door,
And saith—I know you not—to them?
I see the wounded hands and side,
The brow thorn-tortured long ago:
Yea; This Who grieved and bled and died,
This same is He Who must condemn;
He called, but they refused to know;
So now He hears their cry no more.

'BEFORE THE PALING OF THE STARS'

(*Lyra Messianica*, 1864.)

Before the paling of the stars,
  Before the winter morn,
Before the earliest cockcrow,
  Jesus Christ was born:
Born in a stable,
  Cradled in a manger,
In the world His hands had made
  Born a stranger.

Priest and king lay fast asleep
  In Jerusalem,
Young and old lay fast asleep
  In crowded Bethlehem:
Saint and Angel, ox and ass,
  Kept a watch together
Before the Christmas daybreak
  In the winter weather.

Jesus on His Mother's breast
  In the stable cold,
Spotless Lamb of God was He,
  Shepherd of the fold:
Let us kneel with Mary maid,
  With Joseph bent and hoary,
With Saint and Angel, ox and ass,
  To hail the King of Glory.

EASTER EVEN

(*Lyra Messianica*, 1864.)

THERE is nothing more that they can do
For all their rage and boast;
Caiaphas with his blaspheming crew,
Herod with his host,

Pontius Pilate in his Judgement-hall
Judging their Judge and his,
Or he who led them all and passed them all,
Arch-Judas with his kiss.

The sepulchre made sure with ponderous Stone,
Seal that same stone, O Priest;
It may be thou shalt block the holy One
From rising in the east:

Set a watch about the sepulchre
To watch on pain of death;
They must hold fast the stone if One should stir
And shake it from beneath.

God Almighty, He can break a seal
And roll away a Stone,
Can grind the proud in dust who would not kneel,
And crush the mighty one.

. . . .

There is nothing more that they can do
For all their passionate care,
Those who sit in dust, the blessed few,
And weep and rend their hair:

Peter, Thomas, Mary Magdalene,
The Virgin unreproved,
Joseph, with Nicodemus, foremost men,
And John the Well-beloved,

Bring your finest linen and your spice,
Swathe the sacred Dead,
Bind with careful hands and piteous eyes
The napkin round His head;

Lay Him in the garden-rock to rest;
Rest you the Sabbath length:
The Sun that went down crimson in the west
Shall rise renewed in strength.

God Almighty shall give joy for pain,
Shall comfort him who grieves:
Lo! He with joy shall doubtless come again,
And with Him bring His sheaves.

PARADISE: IN A DREAM

(*Lyra Messianica*, second edition, 1865.)

Once in a dream I saw the flowers
That bud and bloom in Paradise;
More fair they are than waking eyes
Have seen in all this world of ours.
And faint the perfume-bearing rose,
And faint the lily on its stem,
And faint the perfect violet
Compared with them.

I heard the songs of Paradise:
  Each bird sat singing in his place;
  A tender song so full of grace
It soared like incense to the skies.
Each bird sat singing to his mate
  Soft cooing notes among the trees:
The nightingale herself were cold
    To such as these.

I saw the fourfold River flow,
  And deep it was, with golden sand;
  It flowed between a mossy land
Which murmured music grave and low.
It hath refreshment for all thirst,
  For fainting spirits strength and rest:
Earth holds not such a draught as this
    From east to west.

The Tree of Life stood budding there,
  Abundant with its twelvefold fruits;
  Eternal sap sustains its roots,
Its shadowing branches fill the air.
Its leaves are healing for the world,
  Its fruit the hungry world can feed,
Sweeter than honey to the taste
    And balm indeed.

I saw the gate called Beautiful;
  And looked, but scarce could look, within;
  I saw the golden streets begin,
And outskirts of the glassy pool.

Oh harps, oh crowns of plenteous stars,
  Oh green palm-branches many-leaved—
Eye hath not seen, nor ear hath heard,
    Nor heart conceived.

I hope to see these things again,
  But not as once in dreams by night;
  To see them with my very sight,
And touch, and handle, and attain:
To have all Heaven beneath my feet
  For narrow way that once they trod;
To have my part with all the Saints,
    And with my God.

WITHIN THE VEIL

(*Lyra Messianica*, second edition, 1865.)

She holds a lily in her hand,
Where long ranks of Angels stand,
A silver lily for her wand.

All her hair falls sweeping down;
Her hair that is a golden brown,
A crown beneath her golden crown.

Blooms a rose-bush at her knee,
Good to smell and good to see:
It bears a rose for her, for me;

Her rose a blossom richly grown,
My rose a bud not fully blown,
But sure one day to be mine own.

PARADISE: IN A SYMBOL

(*Lyra Messianica*, second edition, 1865.)

Golden-winged, silver-winged,
  Winged with flashing flame,
Such a flight of birds I saw,
  Birds without a name:
Singing songs in their own tongue
  (Song of songs) they came.

One to another calling,
  Each answering each,
One to another calling
  In their proper speech:
High above my head they wheeled,
  Far out of reach.

On wings of flame they went and came
  With a cadenced clang,
Their silver wings tinkled,
  Their golden wings rang,
The wind it whistled through their wings
  Where in Heaven they sang.

They flashed and they darted
  Awhile before mine eyes,
Mounting, mounting, mounting still
  In haste to scale the skies—
Birds without a nest on earth,
  Birds of Paradise.

Where the moon riseth not,
  Nor sun seeks the west,
There to sing their glory
  Which they sing at rest,
There to sing their love-song
  When they sing their best:

Not in any garden
  That mortal foot hath trod,
Not in any flowering tree
  That springs from earthly sod,
But in the garden where they dwell,
  The Paradise of God.

AMOR MUNDI

(*The Shilling Magazine*, 1865.)

'Oh, where are you going with your love-locks flowing
  On the west wind blowing along this valley track?'
'The downhill path is easy, come with me an' it please ye,
  We shall escape the uphill by never turning back.'

So they two went together in glowing August weather,
  The honey-breathing heather lay to their left and right;
And dear she was to doat on, her swift feet seemed to float on
  The air like soft twin pigeons too sportive to alight.

'Oh, what is that in heaven where grey cloud-flakes are seven,
Where blackest clouds hang riven just at the rainy skirt?'
'Oh, that 's a meteor sent us, a message dumb, portentous,—
An undecipher'd solemn signal of help or hurt.'

'Oh, what is that glides quickly where velvet flowers grow thickly,
Their scent comes rich and sickly?'—'A scaled and hooded worm.'
'Oh, what 's that in the hollow, so pale I quake to follow?'
'Oh, that 's a thin dead body which waits th' eternal term.'

'Turn again, O my sweetest,—turn again, false and fleetest:
This way whereof thou weetest I fear is hell's own track.'
'Nay, too steep for hill-mounting,—nay, too late for cost-counting:
This downhill path is easy, but there 's no turning back.'

WHO SHALL DELIVER ME?

(*The Argosy*, Feb. 1866.)

God strengthen me to bear myself;
That heaviest weight of all to bear,
Inalienable weight of care.

All others are outside myself;
I lock my door and bar them out,
The turmoil, tedium, gad-about.

I lock my door upon myself,
And bar them out; but who shall wall
Self from myself, most loathed of all?

If I could once lay down myself,
And start self-purged upon the race
That all must run! Death runs apace.

If I could set aside myself,
And start with lightened heart upon
The road by all men overgone!

God harden me against myself,
This coward with pathetic voice
Who craves for ease, and rest, and joys:

Myself, arch-traitor to myself;
My hollowest friend, my deadliest foe,
My clog whatever road I go.

Yet One there is can curb myself,
Can roll the strangling load from me,
Break off the yoke and set me free.

IF

(*The Argosy*, March 1866.)

IF he would come to-day, to-day, to-day,
  O, what a day to-day would be!
But now he 's away, miles and miles away
  From me across the sea.

O little bird, flying, flying, flying
  To your nest in the warm west,
Tell him as you pass that I am dying,
  As you pass home to your nest.

I have a sister, I have a brother,
  A faithful hound, a tame white dove;
But I had another, once I had another,
  And I miss him, my love, my love!

In this weary world it is so cold, so cold,
  While I sit here all alone;
I would not like to wait and to grow old,
  But just to be dead and gone.

Make me fair when I lie dead on my bed,
  Fair where I am lying:
Perhaps he may come and look upon me dead—
  He for whom I am dying.

Dig my grave for two, with a stone to show it,
  And on the stone write my name:
If he never comes, I shall never know it,
  But sleep on all the same.

TWILIGHT NIGHT

(*The Argosy*, Jan. 1868.)

I

We met, hand to hand,
  We clasped hands close and fast,
As close as oak and ivy stand;
  But it is past:
  Come day, come night, day comes at last.

We loosed hand from hand,
  We parted face from face;
Each went his way to his own land
  At his own pace,
  Each went to fill his separate place.

If we should meet one day,
  If both should not forget,
We shall clasp hands the accustomed way,
  As when we met
  So long ago, as I remember yet.

II

Where my heart is (wherever that may be)
  Might I but follow!
If you fly thither over heath and lea,
O honey-seeking bee,
  O careless swallow,
Bid some for whom I watch keep watch for me.

Alas! that we must dwell, my heart and I,
So far asunder.
Hours wax to days, and days and days creep by;
I watch with wistful eye,
I wait and wonder:
When will that day draw nigh—that hour draw nigh?

Not yesterday, and not, I think, to-day;
Perhaps to-morrow.
Day after day 'to-morrow' thus I say:
I watched so yesterday
In hope and sorrow,
Again to-day I watch the accustomed way.

INDEX OF TITLES

INDEX OF FIRST LINES